A BOOK OF EPITAPHS

R. I. P.   1967

A BOOK

OF

EPITAPHS

by

Raymond Lamont Brown

★

Cover design and line whimsies by Ernest Petts

DAVID & CHARLES . NEWTON ABBOT

1969

7153 4171 5

©

RAYMOND LAMONT BROWN

1967, 1969

First published 1967
Second impression 1969

Printed in Great Britain by
Redwood Press Limited Trowbridge Wiltshire
for David & Charles (Publishers) Limited
South Devon House Railway Station
Newton Abbot Devon

Contents

5

Acknowledgements

The author would like to thank the staff of the Central Public Library, Dewsbury, for their patience and help in searching for the more obscure epitaphs. And to all the countless people who have brought to his attention the little-known epitaphs which appear in this book.

Further and particular thanks are offered to the Lord Bishop of Wakefield for kindly contributing an Introduction to the book.

Introduction

This is a most delicious piece of research. Mr Brown has roamed wide and far, and brought to the work of detection a tact, a humour, a sympathy and a historical sense all of which combine to make a power of selection from this rich material of epitaphs, such as to afford the reader greater delight than could be imagined from the title.

The great, the simple, the naughty, the wise, the unfortunate are all represented here. We travel from Mirfield (Robin Hood) to Missolonghi (Byron), from Leeds (Jollity) to the young unmarried girls at Lloughor, Glamorgan.

I am particularly intrigued by Byron's lines on Joseph Blackett, poet and shoemaker of Seaham, Co Durham, where I was born. A classic example of the art of the epitaph in poetry.

Congratulations to Mr Brown for a first-rate job, calculated to amuse many, instruct some, and bring a balanced outlook, on what must come to us all, to everybody who will keep this anthology beside them.

✠ JOHN, WAKEFIELD

June 1967

Author's Preface

This selection of epitaphs has been planned to show as many of man's emotions as possible, so that we have a book of laughter and tears, courage and cowardice, confidence and fear, sentiment and piety, irony and wisdom, wit and humour. Its main purpose is to interest and to entertain, and from the beginning of time man has been interested in his past no less than his future, spending much time and effort in studying the history of his ancestors.

To achieve a balance of subject matter, much editing has been needed and much has been discarded from the mountain of recorded epitaphs available. This book does not, therefore, in any way claim to be an exhaustive work on its subject.

One might think that levity, laughter, spite and malice were hardly to be considered as fit subjects for tombstones, yet a surprising number of epitaphs are to be found in such a vein around the world. In fact, some of the wittiest and most outrageous verses of all have been found in graveyards.

As a secondary theme, and without pretensions to erudition, this book also sets out to explain the development of the epitaph, what to look for and where to find it. Fortunately, the field is almost inexhaustible and there is much of interest that the reader can still discover for himself.

RAYMOND LAMONT BROWN

Dewsbury, Yorkshire
June 1967

Tribute to Pluto

In the mythological age of the gods, the world was divided into regions, each ruled by a god. The Infernal Regions, Hades, Death and Cemeteries fell to the governance of Pluto, son of Cronus and Rhea. As a reward for this rather solemn benefice, he was given the guardianship of riches, of all the precious metals and stones that are buried deep in the earth.

The appearance of Pluto on earth was never a happy event, for his mission was always to take back to his kingdom the spirits of the dead. Riding up from the bowels of the earth in a chariot drawn by four coal-black steeds, he inspired fear in the hearts of men.

Pluto's kingdom was almost impossible to reach without his permission, for it lay deep in the underworld guarded by huge Cerberus, the three-headed dog. Near Pluto's throne were placed the seats of his three judges, Aeacus, Minos and Rhadamanthus, who closely questioned the newly-arrived souls. These hearings were enacted before Themis, the blindfolded, impartial goddess, whose sword of justice hung above the new arrivals. If the souls were proved good, they were led away to the Elysian Fields; if not, they were forever committed to the infernal regions of Tartarus. While the souls were being judged, Pluto, it is said, amused himself by writing their epitaphs. One wonders how many of the following were his handiwork.

Talking About Epitaphs

Of all countries in the world, Great Britain has perhaps the finest collection of folk-lore, country tales and historical relics, and no other nation has a keener sense of its history. Every weekend thousands of people set out to explore the glories of the British heritage. Each person, or group of persons, has his own particular interest and many more every year are discovering the past in the form of epitaphs and so tapping a rich source of social history.

For an epitaph is more than a memorial to the dead, in so much that it is all things to all men. Weever in his *Funerall Monuments* of 1631 writes:

> Of all funerall honours (saith Camden) Epitaphs have always been most respective; for in them love was shewn to the deceased, memorie was continued to posterity, friends were comforted, and the Reader put in minde of Human frailtie.

Whereas in erecting a monument to his parents, Sir Charles Grandison had this to say:

> I will have an elegant, but not sumptuous, monument erected to the memory of both, with a modest inscription, that rather be matter of instruction to the living, than a panegyrick on the departed.

The earliest surviving epitaphs are probably those inscribed upon the tombs of the Ancient Egyptians. Plutarch could not have been further from the truth when he wrote in his *Moralia*, 'What difficulty is there about refraining from reading the inscriptions on tombs as we journey along the roads? . . . Nothing useful or pleasant has been written there.' How wrong he was. Let us look again at Ancient Egypt. The epitaphs of the Pharaohs have added much to our understanding of their ancient culture. Take, for instance, the epitaph of Pharaoh Amenemhet, founder of the Twelfth Dynasty, 2000 B.C.:

> . . . he restored that which he found ruined; that which a city had taken from its neighbour; while he caused city to know its boundary with city, establishing their landmarks like the heavens, distinguishing their waters according to what was in the writings, investigating according to that which was of old, because he so greatly loved justice. (Breasted's translation)

Or again, we read of a Pharaoh's vizier that he was:

> Rekhimire . . . born of Bet and begotten of the *w'b* priest of Amun, Nefer-weben, son of the Mayor and Vizier, Amotu, enjoying the sight of the cows, delighting in the work of the fields and beholding the work of the seasons, summer and winter. . . .

Ancient Egyptian epitaphs always told you more than name, rank and number.

Ancient Greek epitaphs, on the other hand, are of greater literary interest for they have a richness of expression and are often epigrammatic; some are elegiac, some are in verse. In ancient Sparta, epitaphs were only inscribed upon the tombs of those who had distinguished themselves in battle, whereas Roman epitaphs were classless and recorded facts of birth and death rather than eulogies.

Perhaps three of the most important things about epitaphs are that, (*a*) they record the continuity of life, (*b*) they tell us much about the occupations of people living in that district, and (*c*) they mirror the social scene.

First, three examples of (*a*), the continuity of life.

INFANCY

—From the Vavasour tablet in the Belfry Church, York.

How vain a thing is man,
When God thinks meet
Oftimes with swaddling clothes
To join the winding sheet.
A web of forty weeks
Spun forth in pain,
To his dear parents' grief
Soon ravelled out again,
This babe, intombed
Upon the world did peep,
Disliked it, clos'd its eyes,
Fell fast asleep.

CHILDHOOD

—From York Minster.

To Eleazer Clenn. Died of cholera in 1832, aged 6.

This lovely bud, so young and fair,
Call'd hence by early doom,
Just came to show how sweet a flower,
In Paradise should bloom.

YOUTH

To Alicia Iveson. Died aged 23.

Wit join'd to beauty and with virtue crown'd,
Makes woman lovely—all in her were found.

And one example of (*b*), the occupations.

TAILOR, SOLDIER, PARISH CLERK

—The epitaph of an inhabitant of Weston.

Here lies entomb'd within this vault so dark,
A tailor, cloth-drawer, soldier, and parish clerk;
Death snatch'd him hence, and also from him took
His needle, thimble, sword, and prayer-book.
He could not work, nor fight—what then?
He left the world, and faintly cried, 'Amen'!

And, representative of (c), as a mirror of the social scene, this epitaph from the tomb of the murdered sailor at Thursley, Surrey.

> When pitying eyes to see my Grave shall come,
> And with a generous Tear bedew my Tomb,
> Here shall they read my melancholy Fate,
> With Murder and Barbarity complete,
> In perfect Health and in Flower of Age,
> I fell a victim to three Ruffians' Rage.
> On bended Knees, I mercy strove t' obtain,
> Their thirst of Blood made all entreaties vain,
> No dear Relation or still dearer Friend,
> Weeps my hard Lot, or miserable end,
> Yet o'er my Sad Remains (my Name unknown),
> A generous Public have inscribed this Stone.

The actual date when epitaphs first began to lie is uncertain, but many have commented upon their untruths. Thus H. D. Thoreau: 'The rarest thing in an epitaph is truth. . . . Fame itself is but an epitaph, as late, as false, as true.' And Thomas Fuller: 'In some Monuments, the red veins in the marble may seem to blush at the falsehoods written on it. He was a witty man that first taught a stone to speak, but was a wicked one that taught it first to lie.'

How Epitaphs Developed

The earliest tombs to be found in parish churches in this country are those of the twelfth century which were marked by simple stone slabs. At that time, burials inside churches were mainly reserved for the ecclesiastics and abbots. By the thirteenth century, the recumbent effigy had made its appearance. These tombs, with their simple Latin inscriptions, tell us much about the dress, armour and heraldry of the time. By the fourteenth century, a step further had been taken with the introduction of the richly-carved, stone canopy. The setting up of these early tombs and epitaphs, of which only a few now remain, was a major source of employment for many craftsmen during the Middle Ages.

The main materials used were Purbeck and Frosterley marbles, free-stones, sandstones, chalk and Beer-stone, alabaster, wood, laton and bronze. Much of the original decoration and gilt work has now gone.

The epitaphs of medieval times were usually in the form of tender prayers, whereas those of the Elizabethan and Jacobean ages were more often historical and described who a person was and what he did. From 1600 to the Civil War, epitaphs were poetic, changing to brief inscriptions under the Commonwealth. From 1660 to 1680, they became long-winded.

Looking for Epitaphs

It is not a platitude to say that the richest source of epitaphs is in a graveyard, for epitaphs seem to crop up in the most unlikely places. Sometimes epitaphs got no further than the writing of them, and perhaps that said to have been written of Frederick, Prince of Wales, by his father King George II, is the one most full of an unnatural hatred. 'I have lost my eldest son,' the monarch proclaimed, 'and I am glad.'

The oldest graves are to be found in the south part of a churchyard, as it was the custom to avoid the shadow of the church falling across the graves. For in the shadows lurked the Devil and, as every good man and woman knew, the Devil always rode in from the north. In Victorian times, the extreme north side of the churchyard was reserved for suicides.

Very often, you will find that the ground of the south side of a church is higher than the road and even higher than the church foundations themselves; this is because it was the medieval custom to bury the dead one on top of the other *ad infinitum*. Burial normally took place with the head to the west, facing towards the traditional 'Land of the Dead', the eyes facing towards the east and the rising sun.

Tombstones come in many shapes and sizes and the earliest will now be very worn indeed. The familiar table tombs are found both inside the church and out; shaped roughly like an altar, they are nearly always near to the church door. In former times, men and women of charitable disposition would leave money in their wills for bread and beer to be bought for distribution to the poor and this was then set out on the table tombs. In Georgian and Victorian times, table tombs were often raised on legs, and appalling ugly many of them were!

Early headstones were usually thick and dumpy and these were often carved with the emblems of death and immortality—the skull and cross-bones (not only for pirates!), the 'all-seeing eye' surrounded by a snake or serpent, the hourglass, the scythe, the book and quill of the Recording Angel, and the inverted torch, a favourite symbol of death and darkness. Often the tools of a person's trade were carved on his tombstone, the hammer, the saw, the hay-rake, and so on.

In some places, where climatic conditions are conducive, old wooden grave-boards survive, but in our wet northern hemisphere they are soon destroyed. One sometimes finds, particularly in Sussex, Surrey and Kent, instances of iron having been used for headstones.

Humour in the Churchyard

Levity in the churchyard may seem strange to us now, but the custom of using churchyards for sport, markets and pleasure was an old-established and persistent one. There are records as early as the fourth century of St Basil protesting against the holding of markets in churchyards on the pretext of making preparations for festivals. But even though such dignitaries as the canons of the Synod of Exeter of 1287 strictly asked their parish priests to make sure that 'combats, dances, or other improper sports . . . or stage plays or farces' (*ludos theatrales et ludebriorum spectacula*) were prohibited, the fairs persisted and often ale was brewed on the church premises.

Understanding Epitaphs

Deciphering old epitaphs can often be difficult and the following information may be of some assistance.

The tombstone from Roman Caerleon (*Isca Silurum*) is a good example of what to expect in Romano-British graveyards:

'To Gaius Valerius Victor, standard-bearer of the 2nd Legion, Augusta.

```
            D.              M.
      G. VALERIUS.     C.    F.
         GALERIA     VICTOR
    LVGDVNI.  SIG.  LEG II. AV C.
    STP  .XV,  II-ANNOR. XLV. CV.
```

Many Roman epitaphs to be found in Britain begin with
D.M., or D.M.S.—*Dis Manibus*, or *Diis Manibus Sacrum*—
'dedicated to the souls of the departed', or *Siste (Aspice) Victor*
—'Stop, passer-by', or *Sit tibi terra levis*—'May the earth be
light upon thee'. Whereas later tomb inscriptions in Latin
begin *Hic Jacet*—Here lies'.

The phraseology of the early epitaphs is virtually the same.
From the prayer altar of a Roman officer, set up on the Stanhope
moors in Weardale, Durham:

> Sacred to the Invincible Silvanus; Gaius Tetius
> Veturius Micianus, Commandant of Sebosius' Horse,
> set this up gladly, in discharge of his vow, for the cap-
> ture of a magnificent boar, which many before him ha⁴
> failed to catch.

To the pathetic inscription from York:

> To the Gods, the Shades: For Simplicia Forentina,
> a most Innocent Being. Who lived Ten Months. Her
> Father, Felicius Simplex of the 6th Legion, Dedicated
> This.

But remember the pattern:

—From a Roman Burial, Castle Yard, York.

> *DIS   MANIBUS*
> *ET MAEMORIAE (Sic) IVLIAE VICTORINE*
> *QVAE VIXIT ANNOS XXVIIII MENSES II DIES*
> *XV ET CONSTANTIO QVI VIXIT ANNOS IIII*
> *DIES XXI MENSES XI SEPTIMUS LVPIANUS*
> *EX EVOC CONIVGI ET F-IO MEMORIAM*
> *POSSVIT*

To the spirits of the underworld and in memory of
Julia Victorina who lived 29 years, 2 months and 15

days and to Constantius who lived 4 years 21 days and
11 months, Septimus Lupianus centurion *ex evocatis*[1]
placed this memorial to his wife and son.

Useful Words to Remember when Visiting Old Graveyards

A.D.—Anno Domini. In the Year of Our Lord . . .

Ad perpetuam rei memoriam. For a perpetual record of the matter.

Adsum. Here I am.

Aetas suae. Aged . . .

Amicus humani generis. A humanitarian, a philanthropist.

Ars longa, vita brevis. Art is long, life is short.

Beatae memoriae. Of blessed memory.

Caput mortuum. Death head. Residue.

Carpe diem. Enjoy the present day.

Cui Bono? For what good: For whose benefit?

d. Died.

Dabit deus his quoque finem. God will put an end to these also.

Dare vela. To set sail.

Dei gratia. By the grace of God.

Deo volente. D.V. God willing.

Dominus vobiscum. The Lord be with you.

Durante vita. During life.

Elapso tempore. The time having passed.

Errare humanum est. To err is human.

Et sequentes (sequentia). And those that follow.

Et sic de caeteris. And so of the rest.

Ex nihilo nihil fit. Out of nothing nothing is made.

Ex voto. According to one's wishes.

Faber suae fortunae. A self-made man.

Favete linguis. Keep silence.

Fecit. Made it. Executed it.

Fidei defensor. Defender of the faith.

Filius nullius. A son of nobody.

Filius terrae. A son of the soil.

Gloria patri. Glory be to the Father.

Hac voce. Under this word, or phrase.

---

[1] *Ex evocatis*—means that this soldier was promoted to centurion after he had risen through the ranks of the praetorian guard.

Haec olim meminisse juvabit. It will be pleasant hereafter to remember these things.

Hic jacet. Here lies.

Hoc nomine. In this name.

In articulo mortis. At the point of death.

In facie ecclesiae. Before the church.

In futuro. Henceforth.

In memoriam. In memory of . . .

In nomine Domini. In the name of the Lord . . .

In perpetuum. For ever.

In secula seculorum. For ever and ever.

Jubilate Deo. Rejoice in God.

Laus Deo. Praise to God.

Monumentum aere perennius. A monument more lasting than brass.

Mors omnibus communis. Death is common to all.

Natus est. Was born.

Obit. Died.

Pace tua. By your leave.

R.I.P.—Requiescat in pace. May he (she) rest in peace.

Scripta litera manet. The written word remains.

Sic transit gloria mundi. Thus passes away the glory of this world.

Taedium vitae. Weariness of life.

Tempus fugit. Time flies.

Ubi supra. Where above mentioned.

Ut infra. As below.

Ut supra. As above.

Roman Numerals		*Relations*
1	I	*Pater:* Father
2	II	*Socer:* Father-in-law
3	III	*Mater:* Mother
4	IV	*Socrus:* Mother-in-law
5	V	*Filius:* Son
6	VI	*Gener:* Son-in-law
7	VII	*Filia:* Daughter
8	VIII	*Nurus:* Daughter-in-law

Roman Numerals			Relations

9	IX		*Uxor:* Wife
10	X		*Maritus:* Husband
11	XI		*Patrius:* Uncle
12	XII		*Amita:* Aunt
13	XIII		*Consobrinus* ⎫ Cousin (*m.*)
14	XIV		*Consobrina* ⎭ Cousin (*f.*)
15	XV		*Homo:* Man
16	XVI		*Femina:* Woman
17	XVII		*Infans:* Child
18	XVIII		*puer*—Boy
19	XIX		*puella*—Girl
20	XX		*Avus:* Grandfather
30	XXX		*Avia:* Grandmother
40	XL		
50	L		There are alternative Latin
60	LX		words to express the same
70	LXX		relation, but these are the
80	LXXX		most common on epitaphs.
90	XC		

100	C	200	CC
300	CCC	400	CD
500	D	600	DC
700	DCC	800	DCCC
900	CM	1000	M
1500	MD	1800	MDCCC
1900	MCM	2000	MM

Sometimes one will find an epitaph in Latin verse, like this one from the slab tomb of Abbot Shireburn, in Selby Abbey, Yorkshire:

> *In Selby natus, Johannes de Shireburn vocitatus.*
> *Funere prostratus, abbas jacet hic tumulatus:*
> *Annis ter denis notus, vixit bene plenis,*
> *Qui demptis penis, turmis jungatur amaenis.*

Which may be translated:

Born in Selby, John surnamed Shireburn [was]

prostrated by death [and] here [as] Abbot lies buried. Well known for thrice ten years he lived to a good old age, and freed from pains, he is joined to the happy multitudes.

Roman Lettering[1]

A	B	C	D	E	F	G	H	I	J	K	L
⋀	ᘖ	ᘓ	ᗞ	ℰ	ᘖ	ᖆ	(-)	)	)	Ƙ	(
⅄	ᗐ	Ϲ	ʋ	‖	ᖇ	ᖆ	ᐸ	ı	Ŧ		ᚲ
⋀	ᖲ	ᔕ	ᗊ		(	G					ᚲ

M	N	O	P	Q	R	S	T	V	X	Y
⋀	⋀	()	Ϸ	Ϙ	ᖇ	ᔕ	ᘗ	⋁	𝒳	⋎
ᐸ	ᖈ	⟨⟩	Ϸ		ᖈ	Ꙅ	⋎	⋁	𝒳	
⋀	⋀				ᖇ					

A Roman signature: LⅤPⅠⴷNⅤϚ

LUPIANUS.

Runes

Runes were the letters used in the writings of the Northmen and Scandinavians. Very old cemeteries, notably Anglo-Saxon, sometimes have Rune alphabets carved on grave-slabs. Again, our ancestors were very prone to use old grave-slabs to build up walls, or as foundation sets to later buildings.

F	Feh	ᚠ
U	Ur	ᚢ
TH	Thorn	ᚦ
O	Os	ᚾ
R	Raed	ᚱ

[1] Compiled by the author from examples to be found in British Roman occupation sites.

C	Cen	ᚻ
G	Gifu	ᚷ
W	Wen	ᚹ
H	Haegil	ᚺ
N	Naed	ᛏ
I	Is	ᛁ
y	Gaer	ᛟ
I	Ih	ᛆ
P	Peorth	ᛊ
A	Ilcs	ᛦ
S	Sigil	ᛀ
T	Tir	ᛏ
B	Berc	ᛒ
E	Eh	ᛗ
M	Man	ᛘ
L	Lagu	ᛚ
Ng	Ing	ᛉ
D	Daeg	ᛐ
OE	Oethil	ᛟ
AE		ᛡ
St		'ᛉ'

Inscription from an Anglo-Saxon dagger—

+ BIORHTELMMEWORTE

may be translated, 'Biorhtlem made me'.

Inscriptions on Monumental Brasses

Many books have been written on monumental brasses, so let us deal only with the inscriptions and epitaphs.

The inscriptions connected with the early brasses were in Norman French and were set in Lombardic letters around the stonework of the slab mounting.

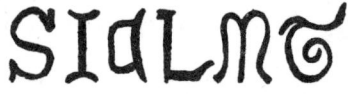

Some Lombardic Letters

From the 1350s, the inscriptions were set out on brass strips, the language used being Latin, with much abbreviation. A common phrase on the mountings was:

Cujus animae propicietur deus, amen.

which was abbreviated to:

Cui.aie.ppict'.ds.Am.

When the inscriptions are placed on the marginal fillet, the corners are usually embossed with the four evangelists' figures, St Mark (the Winged Lion), St Matthew (the Angel), St Luke (the Winged Bull), St John (the Eagle), each figure holding a scroll.

The first use of the English language on brass occurs on the monument to Sir Thomas Walch and his lady. The date is 1393 and the brass is to be found in Wanlip Church, Leicestershire.

It has become a fashion in recent years to take wax rubbings of these monumental brasses and, for those who may be interested in doing so, here is a simple way of obtaining a satisfactory impression.

First clean dust and grit from the surface of the brass you wish to rub. Cover the brass with a tough, though thin paper. Weigh the paper down at each corner and with a piece of heel ball (cobbler's) wax rub the impression of the brass on to the paper. Begin at one end of the brass and work consistently to the end. *Rub only in one direction* for a clear impression. Such a rubbing makes a striking addition to your wall hangings.

How to Date an Epitaph

Dating epitaphs is generally very easy, since most of them have dates carved on them! But it becomes simple to recognize the undated ones by comparing the style with other dated examples.

Finally, before we turn to our collection of epitaphs, a gentle reminder to the few who might, perhaps, forget:

A Reminder

REMEMBER, WHEN YOU ARE EXPLORING FOR EPITAPHS, A CHURCHYARD IS AFTER ALL A *CHURCH*-YARD. TREAT IT WITH REVERENCE AND YOU WILL BE WELCOMED BY THE CHURCH OFFICERS.

Churchyard Humour

FROM THE CHURCHYARD, ABERDEEN

Here lie the bones of Elizabeth Charlotte,
Born a virgin, died a harlot.
She was aye a virgin at seventeen,
A remarkable thing in Aberdeen.

JOHN SIM OF PETERHEAD

Wha lies here?
John Sim, ye needna' speir.
Hullo, John, is that you?
Ay, ay, but I'm deed noo.

THE LLANIDAN CONUNDRUM

Here lies the world's mother,
By nature my aunt—sister to my mother,
My grandmother—mother to my mother,
My great-grandmother—mother to my grandmother,
My grandmother's daughter and her mother.

IN FORFAR CHURCHYARD

'Tis here that Tibby Allan lies,
'Tis here, or here about,
But no one till the Resurrection day,
Shall the very spot dispute.

29

AT REID CHURCHYARD IN THE PARISH OF GAIRTNEY, ANNANDALE

I, Jocky Bell o'Brakenbrow, lyes under this stane,
Five of my awn sons laid it on my wame;
I liv'd aw my days, but sturt or strife
Was man o' my meat, and maister o' my wife;
If you've done better in your time than I did in mine,
Take the stane aff my wame, and lay it on thine.

CULLEN GRAVEYARD, BANFFSHIRE

Here lies interred a man o'micht,
His name was Malcome Downie:
He lost his life ae market nicht
By fa'in aff his pownie.
                    Aged 37 years.

A BEDFORDSHIRE WORTHY
—Luton Parish Church.

Here lies the body of *Thomas Procter*,
Who lived and died without a doctor.

THE LADY OF PEWSEY

Here lies the body of
LADY O'LOONEY
Great-niece of Burke,
commonly called the Sublime.
She was
Bland, passionate, and deeply religious:
Also she painted in water-colours,
And sent several pictures to the Exhibition.
She was first cousin to Lady Jones,
And such is the Kingdom of Heaven.

FROM ST ANDREW'S CHURCHYARD, CAMBRIDGE

Man's life is like a winter's day:
Some only breakfast and away:

Others to dinner stay, and are well fed:
The oldest man but sups, and goes to bed:
Long is his life who lingers out the day,
Who goes the soonest has the least to pay.

AN IRISHMAN'S COMMENT
—Belturbet Churchyard, County Cavan.

Here lies JOHN HIGLEY, whose father and mother were
drowned on their passage from America. Had both lived,
they would have been buried here.

THE WIDOW'S HOPE
—St Michael's Churchyard, Macclesfield.

Mary Broomfield
Dyd 19 Novr, 1755, aged 80.

The chief concern of her life for the last twenty-five years was
to order and provide for her funeral. Her greatest pleasure was
to think and talk about it. She lived many years on a pension
of 9d per week, and yet she saved £5, which at her own request
was laid out on her funeral.

THE WISH OF THE LIVING
—From St Agnes's Churchyard, Cornwall.

Here lies the body of Joan Carthew,
Born at St Columb; died at St Cue:
Children she had five,
Three dead and two alive:
Those that are dead choosing rather
To die with their mother than live with their father.

A DISMAL STORY FROM PENTEWAN, CORNWALL

In this here grave ye see before ye,
Lies buried up a dismal story;
A young maiden she wor crossed in love,
And tooken to the realms above.
But he that crossed her I should say,
Deserves to go t'other way.

FROM A LOVING WIFE

—Wrexham Churchyard.

RICHARD KENDRICK
Was buried August 29th, 1785,
By the desire of his wife,
MARGARET KENDRICK,

IT'S ALL THE SAME!

—Kingsbridge, Devonshire.

Here I lie, at the chancel door,
Here I lie, because I'm poor:
The farther in the more you pay,
Here I lie as warm as they.

MR DAY FROM POOLE

As long as can be,
So long so long was he;
How long, how long, dost say?
As long as the longest DAY.

THE GOODMAN OF WYKE REGIS

Here lies a man by all good men esteemed
Because they proved him really what he seemed.
Faith, hope, and resignation filled his breast;
Good ground we therefore have to think he's blest.

THE TALL MAN FROM DUMFRIES

Here lies Andrew MacPherson,
Who was a peculiar person;
He stood six foot two
Without his shoe,
And he was slew,
At Waterloo.

ROBERT TROLLOPE OF GATESHEAD

Here lies *Robert Trollope*,
Who made your stones roll up.

When Death took his soul up,
His body fill'd this hole up.

JUST ENOUGH

Poems and epitaphs are but stuff:
Here lies ROBERT BURROWS, that's enough.

TO MEET AGAIN
—From West Churchyard, Tranent, East Lothian.

William Matthieson here lies,
Whose age was forty-one;
February seventeenth he dies,
Went Is'bel Mitchell from.
Who was his married wife,
The fourth part of his life.
The soul it cannot die,
Tho' th' body be turn'd to clay;
Yet meet again must they
At the last day.
Trumpets shall sound, archangels cry,
Come forth Is'bel Mitchell and meet
William Matthieson in the sky.

THE PRICE OF PRAYER

Here lyeth the Body of DANIEL JEFFREY.
He was buried ye 22 day of September, 1746,
in ye 18th year of his age.

This youth, when in his sickness lay,
Did for the Minister send, that he would
Come and With him Pray, But he would not atend [*sic*];
But when this young man Buried was
The Minister did him admit he should be
Carried into Church, that he might money get.
By this you See what man will do to get
Money if he can, who did refuse to come
And pray by the foresaid young man.

THE LIGHTNING CONDUCTOR
—Great Torrington.

> Here lies a man who was killed by lightning;
> He died when his prospects seemed to be brightening.
> He might have cut a flash in this world of trouble,
> But the flash cut him, and he lies in the stubble.

HUSBANDS AND WIVES

> Martha Blewitt
> of the Swan, Baythorn End of this Parish.
> Buried 7th May, 1681.
> Was the wife of nine husbands
> Successively, but the 9th outlived her.
> The text to her Funeral Sermon was,
> 'Last of all Women died also.'

—From Chelmsford, Essex.

> *Here lies the man Richard,*
> And Mary his wife
> Whose surname was Prichard
> They lived without strife
> And the reason was plain
> They abounded in riches
> They had no care nor pain
> And his wife wore the breeches.

AN AUNTIE FROM CRAIL, FIFESHIRE

> Here lies my good and gracious Auntie,
> Wham Death has packed in his portmanty,
> Threescore and ten years God did gift her,
> And here she lies, wha de'il daurs lift her?

FROM PAINSWICK CHURCHYARD, STROUD, GLOUCESTER-SHIRE

> My wife lies dead, and here she lies,
> Nobody laughs and nobody cries:

Where she is gone to and how she fares,
Nobody knows and nobody cares.

FROM A COUNTRY CHURCHYARD

Here lies two babbies, dead as nits,
Who died while eating cherry bits,
They were too good to live with we,
So God did take to live with He.

BACKCHAT FROM HEREFORD CHURCHYARD

Grieve not for me, my husband dear,
I am not dead but sleeping here,
With patience wait, prepare to die,
And in short time you'll come to I.

To which the husband carved below:

I am not grieved, my dearest wife,
Sleep on I've got another wife.
Therefore I cannot come to thee,
For I must go and live with she.

THE CHURCHYARD OF ST ALBANS

Sacred to the memory of Martha Gwynn,
Who was so very pure within,
She burst the outer shell of sin,
And hatched herself a cherubim.

A TEAR IN SANTON CHURCHYARD, ISLE OF MAN

Here, friend, is little Daniel's tomb—
To Joseph's age he did arrive.
Sloth killing thousands in their bloom,
While labour kept poor Dan alive,
How strange, yet true, full seventy years
Was his wife happy in her tears!

DANIEL TEAR died 9th December 1707.
Aged 110 years.

THE GLUTTON OF SKYE

Here lie the bones,
O Tonald Jones,
The wale o'men
For eating scones.
Eating scones
And drinking yill,
Till his last moans
He took his fill.

THERE WAS AN OLD LADY FROM RYDE
—Ryde Churchyard.

There was an old lady from Ryde
Who ate some apples and dyed.
The apples fermented inside the lamented
Made cider inside her inside.

FROM A CHURCHYARD IN LIVERPOOL

Poor John lies buried here:
Although he was both hale and stout,
Death stretched him on the bitter bier,
In another world he hops about.

GRANTHAM CHURCHYARD, LINCOLNSHIRE

John Palfreyman, who lyeth here,
Was aged four and twenty year:
And near this place his mother lies,
Also his father, when he dies.

A GRATEFUL NEPHEW
—From Kirton Churchyard.

My Uncle's name I have
And do enjoy his grave;
Betwixt my Parents dear
My bones are lodged here.

ALONE AT LAST

Here snug in her grave my wife doth lie,
Now she's at rest, and so am I!

A SENSIBLE MAN
—From Newtyle Churchyard, Ruthven, Perthshire.

Here lies the body of Robert Small,
Who, when in life, was thick not tall;
But what's of greater consequence,
He was endowed with good sense.

FROM FROME CHURCHYARD

Reader, Death took me without any warning,
I was well at night and died in the morning.

A MUM FROM WOLSTANTON, STAFFORDSHIRE

Some have children, some have none:
Here lies the mother of twenty-one.

OBIT 1690

Here lie the bones,
Of JOSEPH JONES,
Who ate whilst he was able:
But, once o'erfed,
He dropped down dead,
And fell beneath the table.
When from this tomb,
To meet his doom
He rises amidst sinners;
Since he must dwell
In Heaven or Hell,
To take him, which gives best dinners.

TO THE MEMORY OF ELLEN RESON

The charnel mounted on this w
Sets to be seen in funer
A matron plain domestic
In housewifery a princip
In care and pains continu
Not slow, nor gay, nor prodig   } —all.
Yet neighbourly and hospitab
Her children seven yet living
Her sixty-seventh year hence did c
In hope of rise spiritu

THE GRAVE OF THE TWO WIVES OF TOM SEXTON

Here lies the body of Sarah Sexton,
She was a wife that never vexed one;
I can't say as much for the one at the next stone.

MR MILES OF ESHER

This tombstone is a Milestone:
Ha! How so?
Because beneath lies MILES, who's
Miles below.
The smallest grave—The grave of Miles Button, which is
miles in length, Miles in breadth, Miles in depth, and after all
it is only a button-hole!

FROM SUTTON CHURCHYARD

Here lies my poor wife,
Without bed or blankit,
But dead as a door-nail,
God be thankit!

IN DURNESS CHURCHYARD, SUTHERLANDSHIRE

Here doth lye the bodie
Of John Flye, who did die
By a stroke from a sky-rocket,
Which hit him in the eye-socket.

TEAGUE O'BRIEN
—Ballyporien Churchyard, Tipperary, County Tipperary.

> Here I at length repose,
> My spirit now at aise is,
> With the tips of my toes
> And the point of my nose,
> Turned up to the roots of the daisies.

THE WIFE OF JOHN FORD
—Potterne, Wiltshire.

> Here lies Mary, the wife of John Ford,
> We hope her soul is gone to the Lord;
> But if for Hell she has chang'd this life
> She had better be there than be John Ford's wife.

JOLLITY IN LEEDS

> Here lies my wife,
> Here lies she;
> Hellelujah!
> Hallelujee!

FROM ST MICHAEL'S CHURCHYARD, DUMFRIES

> Here lyes Bedal Willy Smyth,
> Wha rang the auld kirk bell,
> He buryed thousand in his day,
> And here he lyes himsel'.
> Some say he was a marriyed man,
> Some say he was no,
> But iv he ever had a spouse,
> She's no wi' him below.

THE CATTLE DEALER FROM KIRKMICHAEL

> Here lies the body of Glencorse,
> He went to the borders with two horse,
> He was a sheep and cattle-dealer,
> At last gave up for want of siller.

TREAD SILENTLY

—From Troutbeck, Westmorland.

Here lies a woman,
No man can deny it,
She died in peace, although she lived unquiet;
Her husband prays, if e'er this way you walk,
You would tread softly—if she wake she'll talk.

THE WOODMAN OF OAKHAM

The Lord saw good, I was lopping off wood,
And down fell from the tree,
I met with a check and broke my neck,
And so death lopped off me.

DEAN CHURCHYARD, BOLTON

A ponderous load on me did fall,
And killed me dead against this wall.

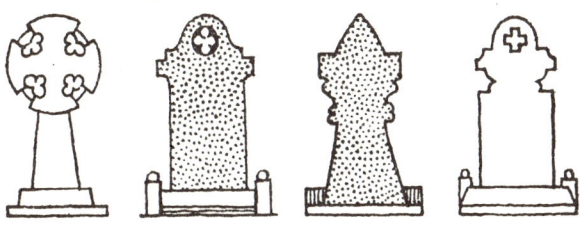

Just for the Famous

Since man first began to carve on stone, famous men and women of the time have been singled out for special epitaphs, of which the following are a selection.

SHAKESPEARE
—Stratford-upon-Avon.

> Good friend, for Jesu's sake forbeare
> To digg the dust enclosed heare;
> Blessed be ye man yt spares these stones,
> And curst be he yt moves my bones.

ETHELBURGA, QUEEN OF THE SAXONS. CIRCA 617 AD

> I was, I am not; smil'd, that since did weep,
> Labour'd, short rest, I walk'd that now must sleep:
> I play'd, I play not; sung, that now am still;
> Saw, that am blind; I would, that have no will;
> I fed that, which feeds worms; I stood, I fell,
> I bade God save you, that now bid farewell.
> I felt, I feel not; follow'd, was pursued;
> I would, have peace; I conquer'd, am subdu'd;
> I moved, want motion; I was stiff that bow
> Below the earth; then something, nothing now.
> I catch'd, am caught. I travelled, here I lie;
> Liv'd in the World, that to the World now die.

41

KING ALFRED, 901 AD

Hail, warlike Alfred, high and noble birth,
Give labour to thine honour, honour to thy worth
Labour procured renown, but joys with grief
Are ever blended; to fear hope brings relief:
To-day of Victor, to-morrow sees thee armed,
The foe though Victor, finds thee still unharmed;
Reeking with sweat thy garb, thy sword with gore,
Prove what a weight you felt the regal power.
No one but thee, through the wild world's domain
Under such toils could rise and breathe again:
Thy sword, though blunted by such bloody strife,
Thou didst not sheathe, nor by it end thy life—
But after many a struggle for thy throne,
Thou found'st peace and life in Christ alone.

DR POTTER, ARCHBISHOP OF CANTERBURY, 1736

Alack and well a-day
Potter himself is turned to clay.

DAVID HUME
—Carlton Hill, Edinburgh.

Within this circular idea,
Call'd vulgarly a tomb,
The ideas and impressions lie,
That constituted Hume.

LORD BYRON

—In the chancel of Hucknall Church, Nottinghamshire.

In the vault beneath,
where many of his ancestors and his
mother are buried
lie the remains of
GEORGE GORDON NOEL BYRON,
Lord Byron of Rochdale
in the County of Lancaster:
The author of 'Childe Harold's Pilgrimage'.
He was born in London on the
22nd of January, 1788;
He died at Missolonghi, in Western
Greece, on the
19th April, 1824.
Engaged in the glorious attempt to
restore that country to her ancient
freedom and renown.
His sister, the Honourable
Augusta Maria Leigh,
placed this tablet to his memory.

ROBIN HOOD

—Kirklees, near Mirfield, Yorkshire.

Hear undernead this latil stean
Laiz Robert Earl of Huntingdon,
Nea arcir ver az hie sa geud,
An pipil kauld him Robin Heud.
Sich atlaz az he an iz men
Vil England nior si agen.
Obit 25 Kalend, Dikimbris, 1247.

CHARLES AND MARY LAMB

—All Saints' Churchyard, Edmonton, North London.

To the Memory of
CHARLES LAMB,
Died 27th Decr. 1834, aged 59.
Farewell dear friend, that smile, that harmless mirth
No more shall gladden our domestic hearth;
That rising tear, that pain forbid to flow,
Better than words no more assuage our woe;
That hand outstretched, from small but well earned store,
Yield succour to the destitute no more.
Yet art thou not all lost; thro' many an age
With sterling sense and humour shall thy page
Win many an English bosom, pleased to see
That old and happier vein revived in thee.
This for our earth, and if with friends we share
Our joys in Heaven, *we hope* to meet thee there.

Also MARY ANNE LAMB,
sister of the above,
Born 3rd Decr 1767, died 20th May 1847.

BEN JONSON (1574–1637). WRITTEN BY ROBERT HERRICK

Here lies Jonson with the rest
Of the poets, but the best.
Reader, woulds't thou more have known?
Ask his story, not the stone;
That will speak what this can't tell
Of his glory; so farewell!

44

DANIEL DEFOE

—Buried in Bunhill Fields, London.

DANIEL DE-FOE.

Born 1661

Died 1731.

Author of

'Robinson Crusoe',

This monument is the result of an appeal

in the 'Christian World' newspaper

to the boys and girls of England for funds

to place a suitable memorial upon the grave

of

DANIEL DE-FOE.

It represents the united contributions

of seventeen hundred persons

Septr 1870.

*And to his 'inspiration' Alexander Selkirk, buried in the Church-
yard of the Island of Juan Fernandez.*

In memory of

ALEXANDER SELKIRK,

Mariner.

A native of Largo, in the county of Fife, Scotland.

Who lived on this island, in complete

solitude, for four years and four months.

He was landed from the 'Cinque Ports' galley,

96 tons, 18 guns, A.D. 1704, and

was taken off in the 'Duke',

privateer, 12th February, 1709.

He died Lieutenant of H.M.S. 'Weymouth',

A.D. 1723, aged 47.

This tablet is erected near Selkirk's lookout

By Commodore Powell and the officers

of H.M.S. 'Topaze', A.D. 1868.

45

THE TOMB OF THE MARTYRS, GREY-FRIARS CHURCHYARD, EDINBURGH

Halt, passenger! take heed what thou dost see,
This tomb doth shew for what some men did die.
Here lies interred the dust of those who stood
'Gainst perjury, resisting unto blood.
Adhering to the covenants and laws,
Establishing the same; which was the cause
Their lives are sacrificed, unto the last
Of Prelatists abjured. Tho' here their dust
Lies mixed with murderers, and other crew,
Whom justice, justly, did to death pursue.
But as for these, in them no cause was found;
Constant and steadfast, zealous witnessing
For the perogative of CHRIST, their king.
Which truths were seal'd by famous GUTHRIE'S head;
And all along to Renwick's blood,
They did endure the wrath of Enemies,
Reproaches, Torments, Deaths and Injuries.
But yet they're these, who from such troubles came,
And now triumph in the glory with the Lamb.

The Covenanters are famous in Scottish history as being the signatories in 1581 of the National Covenant to uphold the Presbyterian religion and the Solemn League and Covenant of 1643. When the Established Church was restored in 1660, the Covenanters refused to recognize the English Church and something like open rebellion broke out in certain of the Scottish counties. Pursued by John Graham of Claverhouse, the Covenanters harried the Government troops up to the fall of the Stuarts in 1688.

ANNE, THE WIFE OF KING JAMES I

Marche with his winde hath strucke a cedar tall
And weeping April mournes the cedar's fall.
And May intends no flowers her month shall bring,
Since she must lose the flower of all the spring.
Thus Marche's winde hath caused April showers
And yet sad May must loose her flower of flowers.

THEODORE, KING OF CORSICA

—St Anne's Churchyard, Soho, erected 1758, by Walpole, Earl of Oxford.

Near this place is interred
THEODORE, KING OF CORSICA
Who died in this parish
December XI, MDCCLVI.,
Immediately after leaving
The King's Bench Prison,
By the benefit of the Act of Insolvency;
In consequence of which
He registered his Kingdom of Corsica
For the use of his creditors.

The grave—great teacher—to the level brings
Heroes and beggars, galley-slaves and kings.

LORD CHIEF JUSTICE MANSFIELD, 1793

Sacred
To the Immortal Memory of
WILLIAM MURRAY, EARL OF MANSFIELD
Late Lord Chief Justice of England,
Who during a course of Thirty Years and upwards, not
only discharged the duties of that high office with un-
exampled assiduity, and unquestionable reputation, but
happily uniting
The Wisdom of Socrates,
The Eloquence of Cicero,
The Harmony of Virgil, and
The Wit and Pleasantries of Horace.

With the Beauties of his own unbounded Genius, became
and was confessedly, the brightest Ornament of Human
Nature that any Age or Country has hitherto been able to
boast of.

The venerable Peer having passed the age of Fourscore,
and finding his corporeal Powers too feeble much longer to
display his wonderful Talents with their wonten Energy,
withdrew himself from the Bench; and willing to appear

47

with those Talents undiminished at the Throne of His
Divine Creator by whom he had been so peculiarly and
abundantly endued, shook off the Clog of Mortality in the
89th year,

And, as an Eagle, wing'd his airy flight
Through Death's pale Shade and all surrounding night,
Up to the happy realms of everlasting Light:
Where, welcom'd by the social Powers Divine,
Freely with them he drinks celestial Wine;
While here, Philosophy remains to mourn
Her Fav'rite fled, fled never to return,
Until his God shall at the Judgment Day,
With his bright soul reanimate his Clay
And all with him to dwell from hence to Heav'n convey.

WILLIAM HUNTINGDON, S.S. OBIT 1813

The epitaph of the famous 'Coalheaver Preacher', buried at
the Chapel, Lewes:

Here lies the Coalheaver,
Belov'd of his God, but abhorred of Men.
The Omniscient Judge at the Grand Assize,
Shall ratify and confirm this
To the confusion of the many thousands;
For England and its Metropolis shall know
That there hath been a prophet among them.

W.H.   S.S. (Sinner Saved)

MRS OLDFIELD, ACTRESS

This we must own in justice to her shade,
'Tis the first bad exit OLDFIELD ever made.

SIR JOHN STRANGE

Here lies an honest lawyer—
That is Strange!

POPE ADRIAN

> *Adrianus, Papa VI, hic situs est*
> *Qui nihil sibi infelicius. In vita*
> *Quam quod imperaret Duxit.*

Pope Adrian VI lies here, who experienced nothing more unhappy in life than that he commanded.

DAVID GARRICK, ACTOR

To paint fair nature, by divine command—
Her magic pencil in his glowing hand—
A Shakespeare rose—then to expand his fame
Wide o'er this 'breathing world', a Garrick came.
Though sunk in death the forms the poet drew,
The actor's genius made them breathe anew;
Though, like the Bard himself, in night they lay,
Immortal Garrick call'd them back today;
And, till Eternity, with power sublime,
Shall mark the mortal hour of hoary Time,
Shakespeare and Garrick like a twin star shall shine.

WILLIAM HOGARTH, PAINTER
—Written by David Garrick, and to be found in Chiswick Churchyard.

Farewell, great painter of mankind,
Who reached the noblest point of art:
Whose pictur'd morals charm the mind,
And, thro' the eye, correct the heart.
If genius fire thee, reader, stay:
If nature touch thee, drop a tear;
If neither move thee, turn away,
For HOGARTH'S honour'd dust lies here.

ALEXANDER THE GREAT

Sufficit huic tumulus cui non sufficeret orbis.
Here a mound suffices for one for whom the world was not
large enough.

JOHN HORNE TOOKE

John Horne Tooke was always considered to be a man of singular tastes, so that his friends and neighbours were not surprised when he announced that he was going to erect his own tomb in his back garden. After weeks of measuring and designing, he set men to work digging and cementing. The tomb consisted of a brick vault built on top of a tumulus in his kitchen garden. The monumental slab at the top, which was to take the epitaph, was of fine, black Irish marble.

John Tooke worked day and night on his last resting place and paid so little attention to food and his health that when he became ill, all his friends thought it was a part of his plan to bring the vault into immediate use. He survived, however, to live several years after—and on his death his executors ordered that he be buried elsewhere! The unused epitaph remained.

JOHN HORNE TOOKE
Late proprietor
And now occupier, of this spot,
was
Born in June 1736, and Died ——
In the —— year of his age.
Contented and grateful.

MY LORD OF ROCHESTER'S EPITAPH

This epitaph was written for King Charles II, by Lord Rochester, on the King's own invitation.

Here lies our Sovereign Lord the King,
Whose word no man relies on;
Who never said a foolish thing,
And never did a wise one.

To which the King replied:
The matter is easily accounted for: my words were my own, my actions were my ministers'.

ALEXANDER WARDLAW

*Chamberlain to the Rt Hon The Earl of Wigtown. Died 15th
March, 1721, aged 67 years.*
—Biggar Churchyard.

Here lyes a man, whose upright heart
With virtue was profusely stor'd,
Who acted well the honest part
Between the tenants and their lord.

Betwixt the sands and flinty rock
Thus steer'd he in the golden mien;
While his blythe countenance bespoke
A mind unsullied and serene.

As to the Bruce the Fleming prov'd
Faithful, so to the Fleming's heir
Wardlaw behav'd, and was belov'd
For justice, candour, faith, and care.

His merit shall preserve his name
To latest ages free from rust,
Till the Archangel raise his frame
To joyn his soul amongst the just.
Hic monumentum posuit Joannes Wardlaw, Alexandri filius.

IN THE CHURCHYARD OF EAST HUCKNALL, THE EPITAPH
OF ONE OF THE DUKE OF DEVONSHIRE'S PARK-KEEPERS

My gun's discharged,
My ball is gone,
My powder's spent,
My work is done.
Those panting deer
I've left behind
May now have time
To gain the wind,
Since I, who oft have
Chased them o'er
The verdant plains,
Am now no more.

51

ON DR LOCKYER, THE PILL INVENTOR, IN THE REIGN OF CHARLES II
—St Saviour's Churchyard, Southwark.

Here Lockyer lies interr'd; enough his name
Speakes, which hath few competitors in fame.
A name, soe great, soe generalle, may scorne
Inscriptions which doe vulgar tombs adorne.
A diminution 'tis, to write in verse
His eulogies, which most men's mouths rehearse.
His virtues and his PILLS are so well knowne
That envy can't confine them under stone,
But they'll survive his dust, and not expire
Till all things else at th' universal fire.
This verse is lost, his PILLS embalms him safe
To future times, without an epitaph.

A JESTER'S EPITAPH

Here lies the Earl of Suffolk's fool,
Men called him DICKY PEARCE:
His folly served to make folks laugh,
When wit and mirth were scarce.
Poor Dick, alas! is dead and gone—
What signifies the cry!
Dickys enough are still behind,
To laugh at by and by.

THE CELEBRATED HIGHWAYMAN
—From Covent Garden Churchyard, the grave epitaph of the celebrated
Claud du Val, highwayman, hanged at Tyburn, 1670.

Here lies Du Vall! Reader, if male thou art
Look to thy purse; if female to thy heart.
Much havick hath he made of both; for all
Men he may stand, and women he may fall.

JOHN DONNE

Clergyman, religious writer, poet, 1573–1631.

> Reader, I am to let thee know,
> Donne's body only lies below;
> For, could the grave his soul comprise,
> Earth would be richer than the skies.

SIR CHRISTOPHER WREN
—St Paul's Cathedral.

> *Si monumentum requiris, circumspice.*
> If you seek his monument, look around you.

SAMUEL FOOTE
—Westminster Abbey.

> Here lies one Foote, whose death may thousands save,
> For death has now one foot within the grave.

THOMAS PARR

Of the County of Salop,
Born *anno* 1483.

> He lived in the Reigns of Ten princes, viz:—
> Edward the 4th, Edward the 5th,
> Richard the 3rd, Henry the 7th,
> Henry the 8th, Edward the 6th,
> Mary, Elizabeth, James and Charles.

He died in London,
Aged 152 years,
And was buried here, November 13th, 1635.

THE LEGH CHAPEL, AT MACCLESFIELD

Here lyeth the bodie of Perkyn a Legh,
That for King Richard the death did dye,
Betrayed for Righteousness;
And the bones of Sir Piers, his son,
That with King Henry V did wonne
In Paris.

In their memory Sir Peter Legh, of Lyme, Kt., descending from them, finding the said old verses written upon a stone in this chapel, did re-edify this place in AD 1626.

FROM SWEETHEART ABBEY, DUMFRIESSHIRE

Composed by Hugh de Burgh, Prior of Lanercost on Devorgilla, who died, 1289, widow of John Baliol.

In Devorvilla moritur sensata Sibilla,
Cum Marthaque pia, contemplativa Maria;
Da Devorvillam requie, Rex summe potiri
Quam tegit iste lapis cor pariterque viri.

In Devorgil, a sybil sage doth die, as
Mary contemplative, as Martha pious;
To her, Oh! deign, high King, rest to impart
Whom this stone covers with her husband's heart.

EPITAPH FOR 'CHING CHING' A MUSICAL GENIUS WHO LIVED IN THE BACK STREETS OF EDINBURGH

In silent rest beneath this green
Here sleepeth sweetly he,
Who in the body on life's scene
Was born a dwarf to be.

But who within this childlike-frame
Display'd a giant mind,
Where fires of genius high did flame,
And love of womankind!

Music to him was bread and drink,
And love the breath of life;
Of discord's jars he scorn'd to think,
And those of hate and strife.

So living, so he pass'd away,
And here his body lies;
His cherub soul, unsmudged with clay,
Soar'd up beyond the skies.

MEMORIAL TO SIR RICHARD WORME, PETERBOROUGH CATHEDRAL

Does Worm eat Worme? Knight Worme this truth confirms,
For here, with worms, lies Worme, a dish for worms.
Does worm eat Worme? Sure Worme will this deny,
For Worme with worms, a dish for worms don't lie.
'Tis so and 'tis not so, for free from worms,
'Tis certain Worme is blest without his worms.

NEAR ROB ROY'S GRAVE, BALQUHIDDER, PERTHSHIRE

Beneath this stane lies Shanet Roy,
Shon Roy's reputed mother;
In all her life this Shon Roy
She never had another.

'Tis here or hereabout, they say,
The place no one can tell;
But when she'll rise at the last day,
She'll ken the stane hersel'.

A COUNTRY CHURCHYARD, NEAR ANCRUM MOOR, ROX-BURGHSHIRE

Fair Maiden Lillard lies under this stane,
Little her stature, but great her fame.
Upon the English louns [fellows, men, soldiers] she laid
many thumps,
And when her legs were cutted off she fought on her
stumps.

SIR THOMAS WOODCOCK

Lord Mayor of London, 1405

Hic Jacet, Tom Shorthose,
Sine tomb, sine sheets, sine riches,
Ni vixit sine gown,
Sine cloak, sine shirt, sine breeches.

THE FORGOTTEN KING

In the churchyard at Wimbledon, Surrey, there is to be
found the epitaph of Don John Emmanuel's (King of Portugal)
natural son, John Martin. To be out of the way, John Martin
was sent to England, where he became a gardener.

Though skilful and experienced,
He was modest and unassuming;
And tho' faithful to his masters,
And with reason esteemed,
He was kind to his fellow-servants,
And was therefore beloved.
His family and neighbours lamented his death,
As he was a careful husband, a tender father, and an honest
man.
He died March 30th, 1760, aged 66.

FROM BRIGHTON CHURCHYARD

On one of his many visits to Brighton, King George IV met a remarkable woman, Phoebe Hessel, and asked her how she supported herself in her old age. The old lady replied that she lived mostly on charity. 'Half a guinea a week,' said she, 'will make me as happy as a princess.' His Majesty ordered that she be paid that amount out of his allowances until she died.

Even in extreme old age she '. . . told capital stories, had an excellent memory, and was in every respect most agreeable company.'

In Memory of Phoebe Hessel, who was born at Stepney, 1713.

She served for many years as a private soldier
In the 5th Regiment of Foot, in different parts
Of Europe and in the Year 1745 fought under the
Command of the Duke of Cumberland at the Battle
Of Fontenoy where she received a bayonet wound
In her arm.
Her long life which commenced in the time of
Queen Anne extended to the reign of George IV,
By whose munificence she received comfort and
Support in her latter years.
She died at Brighton where she had long resided.

December 12th, 1821. Aged 108 years.

BLIND JACK'S EPITAPH

The grave of John Metcalf, 'Blind Jack' of Knaresborough, lies in the churchyard of Spofforth, Yorkshire. John Metcalf lost his sight at the age of six after an attack of smallpox. Undaunted, he pursued a normal life, married, became a soldier and was present on the bloody field of Culloden. After his army career, he was the first to set up in 1754 a stage-wagon between York and Knaresborough, and his uncanny judgement enabled him to take on road-making. When he died in 1801 he had the making of bridges, houses and hundreds of miles of roads in Yorkshire, Lancashire, Cheshire and Derbyshire to his credit.

THE BLIND PATRIOT

OBIT 26th April, 1801. Aged 93.

Here lies JOHN METCALF, one whose infant sight
Felt the dark pressure of an endless night;
Yet such the fervour of his dauntless mind,
His limbs full strung, his spirit unconfined,
That, long ere yet life's bolder years began;
The sightless efforts market th'aspiring man
Not marked in vain—high deeds his manhood dared,
And commerce, travel, both his ardour shared.
'Twas his a guide's unerring aid to lend—
O'er trackless wastes to bid new roads extend;
And, when rebellion reared her giant size,
'Twas his to burn with patriot enterprise;
For parting wife and babes, a pang to feel,
Then welcome danger for his country's weal.
Reader, like him, exert thy utmost talent given!
Reader, like him, adore the bounteous hand of Heaven.

The Epitaphs of Robert Burns

(1759–1796)

Glossary of difficult dialect words which appear in the
Epitaphs of Robert Burns

A': All
Ae: One
Aften: Often
Ain: One's own
Ance: Once
Awa': Away
Banes: Bones
Behint: Behind
Billie: Fellow, brother
Blate: Bashful
Bleth'ran: One who talks a lot
Brunstane: Brimstone
Ca': Call
Carl: Old man
Carlin': Old wife
Cauld: Cold
Coof: Fool
Deil: The Devil
Dool: Sorrow
Fa': Fall
Fu': Full
Gane: Gone
Gie: Give
Gien: Given

Gear: Goods, money, stuff, belongings
Gleg gullie: Sharp knife
Grun: Ground, soil
Glowrin': Glowering
Graff: Grave
Gude: Good
Haud: Hold
Kent: Knew
Mak': Make
Maun: Must
Mixtie-Maxtie: Confused
Nae: None
Nane: None
Neuks: Corners
Ony: Any
O't: Of it
Owre: Over, too
Sair-worn: Service-worn
Saul: Soul
Schulin': Schooling
Sic: Such
Siche: Such
Snool: To cringe, or to snub

Sodger: Soldier	Warl': World
Stanes: Stones	Weans: Small children
Stoppit: Stopped	Weel: Well
Ta'en: Taken	Wha: Who
Tak': Take	Whae'er: Whosoever
Thegither: Together	Whingin': Peevish
Thir: These	Wi': With
Tither: The other	Wi'n: Were
Wad: Would	Wintles (*verb*): To struggle

EPITAPH ON A NOTED COXCOMB

Captain William Roddick of Corbiston.

> Light lay the earth on Billy's breast—
> His chicken heart so tender;
> But build a castle on his head,
> His skull will prop it under.

EPITAPH FOR GAVIN HAMILTON, ESQ

Gavin Hamilton, a lawyer, became acquainted with Burns in the autumn of 1783. At that time they were both at loggerheads with the Kirk and its bigoted minister, the Reverend William 'Daddy' Auld. Hamilton was always a friend of Burns and helped him to sell many copies of his poems in the Kilmarnock Edition.

> The poor man weeps—here Gavin sleeps,
> Whom canting wretches blam'd;
> But with such as he, where'er he be,
> May I be sav'd or damn'd!

EPITAPH FOR ROBERT AIKEN

Robert Aiken, a prosperous and convivial lawyer of the town of Ayr, was a great admirer of Burns's poems.

> Know thou, O stranger to the fame
> Of this much lov'd, much honoured name!
> (For none that knew him need be told)
> A warmer heart Death ne'er made cold.

EPITAPH FOR JESSIE LEWARS

Jessie Lewars, the younger daughter of John Lewars, Supervisor of Excise at Dumfries, was the last of Burns's heroines. During the last six months of Burns's illness Jessie helped to nurse him, and he fancied himself in love with her. She lies buried in St Michael's Churchyard, Dumfries, not far from the grave of Burns. These lines were written by Burns while Jessie suffered from a slight indisposition, 'In case of the worst, Jessie,' joked Burns, 'let me provide you with an epitaph!'

> Say, sages, what's the charm on earth
> Can turn Death's dart aside?
> It is not purity and worth,
> Else Jessie had not died.

EPITAPH FOR WILLIAM CRUICKSHANK

William Cruickshank was sometime Rector of the High School, Canongate, Edinburgh. Later he became the Latin master at Edinburgh High School. Burns lodged with Cruickshank and his family at 2 St James's Square, from the autumn of 1787 to February 1788.

> Honest Will's to Heaven gane,
> And mony shall lament him;
> His faults they a' in Latin lay,
> In English nane e'er kent them.

EPITAPH TO THOMAS SAMSON

Thomas Samson was a well-known seedsman in the town of Kilmarnock, Ayrshire. After a particularly good day out shooting on the moors, Samson told Burns that he would like to be buried on the moors. Burns said he would write an epitaph in readiness.

Tam Samson's weel-worn clay here lies
Ye canting zealots, spare him!
If Honest Worth in Heaven rise,
Ye'll mend or ye wi'n near him.

'But, Rab,' protested Tam, 'I'm no' deid yet!' Burns's quill
scratched the vellum again.

Go, Fame, an' canter like a filly,
Thro', a' the streets an' neuks o' Killie,[1]
Tell ev'ry social, honest billie
To cease his Grievin',
For yet, unskaithed by Death's gleg gullie,
Tam Samson's livin'!

Thomas Samson is buried in the churchyard of Laigh, Kilmarnock, and his seedsman's business still survives.

EPITAPH ON MY EVER-HONOURED FATHER

William Burns[2] (1721–84), the Bard's father, is buried in the
ruined kirkyard of Alloway, Ayrshire. This kirk was the setting
of a powerful scene in Burns's poem 'Tam o' Shanter'.

O ye whose cheek the tear of pity stains,
Draw near with pious rev'rence and attend!
Here lie the loving Husband's dear remains,
The tender Father, and the gen'rous Friend.

The pitying Heart that felt for human Woe;
The dauntless heart that fear'd no human pride;
The Friend of Man, to vice alone a foe;
'For ev'n his failings lean'd to Virtue's side.'[3]

[1] Killie, a word used by the country people for the town of Kilmarnock.
[2] The family name is severally spelt, Burns, Burnes, Burness.
[3] Goldsmith (R.B. 1786).

EPITAPH FOR WILLIAM NICOL, OF THE HIGH SCHOOL, EDINBURGH

Ye maggots, feed on Nicol's brain,
For few sic feasts you've gotten;
And fix your claws in Nicol's heart,
For deil a bit o't's rotten.

EPITAPH ON WILLIAM HOOD, SENIOR, IN TARBOLTON

William Hood was one of the ruling elders of the kirk that levelled its artillery against Burns for his 'immoral indiscretions'.

Here Souter Hood in death does sleep;
To Hell if he's gane thither,
Satan, gie him thy gear to keep;
He'll haud it weel thegither.

EPITAPH ON MY OWN FRIEND AND MY FATHER'S FRIEND, WILLIAM MUIR OF TARBOLTON MILL

William Muir was a man with the proverbial heart of gold; it was he and his family who took Jean Armour into their care when she was pregnant for a second time by Burns.

An honest man here lies at rest,
As e'er God with His image blest;
The friend of man, the friend of truth,
The friend of age, and guide of youth;
Few hearts like his, with virtue warm'd,
Few heads with knowledge so informed;
If there's another world, he lives in bliss;
If there is none, he made the best of this.

EPITAPH ON A HENPECKED COUNTRY SQUIRE

In these three verses Burns was referring to Laird William Campbell of Netherplace, whose farm was next to Burns's property at Mossgiel.

> As father Adam first was fool'd,
> (A case that's still too common,)
> Here lies a man a woman ruled,
> The Devil ruled the woman.

> O Death, hadst thou but spar'd his life,
> Whom we this day lament,
> We freely wad exchanged the wife,
> And a' been weel content.
> E'en as he is, cauld in his graff,
> The swop we yet will do't;
> Tak thou the carlin's carcass aff,
> Thou'se get the saul o'boot.

And the nastiest verse:

> One Queen Artemisia, as old stories tell,
> When deprived of her husband she loved so well,
> In respect for the love and affection he showed her,
> She reduc'd him to dust and she drank up the powder.
> But Queen Netherplace, of a diff'rent complexion,
> When called on to order the fun'ral direction,
> Would have eat her dead lord, on a slender pretence,
> Not to show her respect but—to save the expence!

EPITAPH ON A NOISY POLEMIC

The 'polemic' was James Humphrey, a mason from Mauchline, Ayrshire.

> Below thir stanes lie Jamie's banes;
> O Death, it's my opinion,
> Thou ne'er took such a bleth'ran bitch
> Into thy dark dominion!

EPITAPH ON A WAG IN MAUCHLINE

The epitaph was to James Smith, a draper and crony of Burns's. After his business failed, Smith emigrated to Jamaica.

Lament him Mauchline husbands a',
He aften did assist ye;
For had ye staid whole weeks awa',
Your wives they ne'er had miss'd ye!

Ye Mauchline bairns, as on ye press
To school in bands thegither;
O tread ye lightly on his grass,—
Perhaps he was your faither!

EPITAPH FOR CAPTAIN HENDERSON

A gentleman who held the patent for his honours immediately from Almighty God.

Henderson was an Edinburgh associate of Burns's.

Stop, passenger!—my story's brief,
And truth I shall relate, man;
I tell nae common tale o' grief—
For Matthew was a great man.

If thou uncommon merit hast,
Yet spurn'd at Fortune's door, man;
A look of pity hither cast—
For Matthew was a poor man.

If thou a noble sodger art,
That passest by this grave, man,
There moulders here a gallant heart—
For Matthew was a brave man.

If thou on men, their works and ways,
Canst throw uncommon light, man,
Here lies wha weel had won thy praise—
For Matthew was a bright man.

If thou at Friendship's sacred ca'
Wad life itself resign man,
Thy sympathetic tear maun fa'—
For Matthew was a kind man.

If thou art staunch without a stain,
Like the unchanging blue, man,
This was a kinsman o' thy ain—
For Matthew was a true man.

If thou hast wit, and fun, and fire,
And ne'er gude wine did fear, man,
This was thy billie, dam, and sire—
For Matthew was a queer man.

If any whiggish whingin' sot,
To blame poor Matthew dare, man,
May dool and sorrow be his lot!
For Matthew was a rare man.

EPITAPH FOR A SUICIDE

The only surviving clue to the suicide's identity are the
initials D— C—.

Here lies in earth a root of Hell,
Set by the Diel's ain dibble;
This worthless body damn'd himself',
To save the Lord the trouble.

EPITAPH ON GABRIEL RICHARDSON, BREWER, DUMFRIES

Verse inscribed on a glass goblet.

Here brewer Gabriel's fire's extinct,
And empty all his barrels:
He's blest if—as he brew'd—he drink
In upright, virtuous morals.

EPITAPH FOR MR EBENEZER 'WILLIE' MICHIE, SCHOOL-MASTER OF CLEISH PARISH, FIFESHIRE

Here lie Willie Michie's banes,
O Satan, when ye tak' him,
Gie him the schulin' o' your weans,
For clever DEILS he'll mak' them!

EPITAPH ON HOLY WILLIE

'Holy Willie' was William Fisher, a farmer and elder of the kirk. It was he who pressed the Reverend William 'Daddy' Auld to take proceedings against those who did not attend church regularly. But Fisher, too, fell from grace on a charge of drunkenness.

Here Holy Willie's sair-worn clay
Tak's up its last abode;
His saul has ta'en some other way,
I fear the left-hand road.

Stop! there he is, as sure's a gun,
Poor, silly body, see him!
Nae wonder he's as black's the grun:
Observe wha's standing wi' him.

Your brunstane Devilship, I see,
Has got him there before ye;
But haud your nine-tail cat a wee,
Till ance you've heard my story.

Your pity I will not implore,
For pity ye have nane;
Justice, alas! has gi'en him o'er,
And mercy's day is gane.

But hear me, Sir, Diel as ye are,
Look something to your credit,
A coof like him wad stain your name,
If it were kent ye did it.

EPITAPH ON JOHN BUSHBY

A Dumfries lawyer and County Sheriff-Clerk.

Here lies John Bushby, honest man,
Cheat him, Devil, if you can.

EPITAPH ON JOHN DOVE

Keeper of the Whitefoord Arms, Mauchline.

The Bachelors Club, of which Burns was a member, met at
John Dove's inn.

Here lies Johnnie Pigeon;
What was his religion,
Whae'er desires to ken,
To some other warl',
Maun follow the carl,
For here Johnnie Pigeon had nane!

Strong ale was ablution,
Small beer persecution,
A dram was *momento mori*;
But a full-flowing bowl,
Was the saving his soul,
And port was celestial glory.

EPITAPH FOR MR WALTER RIDDELL

A Dumfries laird whom Burns despised for his lack of spleen.

Sic a reptile was Wat, sic a miscreant slave,
That the worms ev'n damn'd him when laid in his grave;
'In his skull there's a famine,' a starved reptile cries,
'And his heart is rank poison!' another replies.

EXTEMPORE EPITAPH

On a person nicknamed 'The Marquis', who asked Burns to write an epitaph for him.

'The Marquis' was the keeper of a 'respectable public-house', in Dumfries, and the alley in which the inn was situated was called 'The Marquis's Close'.

> Here lies a mock Marquis whose titles were shamm'd
> If ever he rise, it will be to be damned.

EPITAPH ON 'WEE JOHNNIE'

John Wilson printed Burns's first volume of poems, quite unaware that Burns had written this epitaph in his honour.

> *Hic jacet wee Johnnie.*
> Whoe'er thou art, O reader, know,
> That Death has murder'd Johnnie;
> An' here his *body* lies fu' low—
> For *saul* he ne'er had any.

A BARD'S EPITAPH

Burns wrote this poem as a touching 'finis' for his Kilmarnock Edition of July 1786. It is unlikely that he meant it as his own epitaph, for it makes no mention of what was most dear to his heart, his wife Jean—and girls in general!

> Is there a whim-inspir'd fool,
> Owre fast for thought, owre hot for rule,
> Owre blate to seek, owre proud to snool?
>   Let him draw near;
> And o'er this grassy heap sing dool,
>   And drap a tear.

Is there a Bard of rustic song,
Who noteless, steals the crowds among,
That weekly this area throng?
                              O, pass not by!
But, with a frater-feeling strong.
                              Here, heave a sigh.

Is there a man whose judgment clear,
Can others teach the course to steer,
Yet runs, himself, life's mad career,
                              Wild as the wave?
Here pause—and thro' the starting tear,
                              Survey this grave.

The poor Inhabitant below
Was quick to learn and wise to know,
And keenly felt the friendly glow,
                              And softer flame;
But thoughtless follies laid him low,
                              And stain'd his name!

Reader attend—whether thy soul
Soars fancy's flights beyond the pole,
Or darkling grubs this earthly hole,
                              In low pursuit,
Know, prudent, cautious, self-control
                              Is Wisdom's root.

EPITAPH ON CAPTAIN LASCELLES

When Lascelles thought fit from this world to depart,
Some friends warmly thought of embalming his heart;
A bystander whispers—'Pray don't make so much o't,
The subject is poison, no reptile will touch it.'

EPITAPH ON WILLIAM GRAHAM, ESQ, OF MOSSKNOWE

'Stop thief!' Dame Nature call'd to Death,
As Willy drew his latest breath;
My choicest model thou hast ta'en.
How shall I make a fool again?

INSCRIPTION FOR THE HEADSTONE OF FERGUSSON THE POET

Here lies Robert Fergusson
Born Sept 5th, 1751. Died October 16th, 1774.

In 1787, Burns commissioned an architect to erect a stone on Fergusson's grave, after he had received permission to do so from the Bailies of the Canongate Churchyard.

No sculptur'd marble here, nor pompous lay,
'No storied urn nor animated bust';[1]
This simple stone directs pale Scotia's way,
To pour her sorrows o'er her Poet's dust.

These additional verses, not inscribed, appeared in Burns's *Second Commonplace Book.*

She mourns, sweet tuneful youth, thy hapless fate;
Tho' all the powers of song thy fancy fired,
Yet Luxury and Wealth lay by in State,
And thankless, starv'd what they so much admired.

This humble tribute, with a tear, he gives,
A brother Bard—he can no more bestow;
But dear to fame thy Song immortal lives,
A nobler monument than Art can shew.

[1] A line from Gray's 'Elegy'.

EPITAPH ON JOHN RANKINE

John Rankine farmed the Adamhill estate near Tarbolton.

Ae day, as Death, that gruesome carl,
Was driving to the tither warl'
A mixtie-maxtie motley squad,
And mony a guilt-bespotted lad—
Black gowns of each denomination,
And thieves of every rank and station,
From him that wears the star and garter,
To him that wintles in a halter:
Ashamed himself to see the wretches,
He mutters, glowrin' at the bitches,
'By God I'll not be seen behint them,
Nor 'mang the sp'ritual core present them,
Without, at least, ae honest man,
To grace this damn'd infernal clan!'
By Adamhill a glance he threw,
'Lord God!', quoth he, 'I have it now,
There's just the man I want, i'faith!'
And quickly stoppit Rankine's breath.

LINES ON THE AUTHOR'S DEATH

*Written with the supposed view of being handed to John Rankine
after the poet's interment.*

He who of Rankine sang, lies stiff and dead,
And a green grassy hillock hides his head;
Alas; alas; a devilish change indeed.

EPITAPH ON A LAP-DOG

Named Echo.

In wood and wild, ye warbling throng,
Your heavy loss deplore;
Now, half extinct your powers of song,
Sweet Echo is no more.

Ye jarring, screeching things around,
Scream your discordant joys;
Now, half your din of tuneless sound
With Echo silent lies.

EPITAPH TO SWEARING BURTON

Burton was a dandy whom Burns once met.

Here cursing, swearing Burton lies,
A buck, a beau, or 'Dem my eyes!'
Who in his life did little good,
And his last words were 'Dem my blood'.

EPITAPH ON JAMES GRIEVE, LAIRD OF BOGHEAD, TAR-BOLTON

Here lies Boghead amang the dead,
In hopes to get salvation;
But if such as he in Heav'n may be,
Then welcome, hail! damnation.

EPITAPH ON GRIZZEL GRIMME

Here lyes with Dethe auld Grizzel Grimme,
Lincluden's[1] ugly wiche;
O Dethe, an' what a taste hast thou
Cann lye with sich a bitche!

BURNS'S OWN EPITAPH

Robert Burns died at his own house in Dumfries on 21 July
1796, at the age of 37. He was given a funeral with military
honours and was buried in a corner of St Michael's Churchyard,
Dumfries. In 1815, Burns was reinterred in a specially-built
mausoleum, paid for out of public subscription, at a cost of
around £1,500.

[1] Lincluden is in Kirkcudbrightshire, on the western outskirts of
Dumfries, famous for its abbey and college.

Consigned to earth, here rests the lifeless clay,
Which once a vital spark from heaven inspired!
The lamp of genius shone full bright as day,
Then left the world to mourne its light retired.
While beams that splendid orb which lights the sphere,
While mountain streams descend to swell the main,
While changeful seasons mark the rolling years—
Thy fame, O Burns, let Scotia still retain.

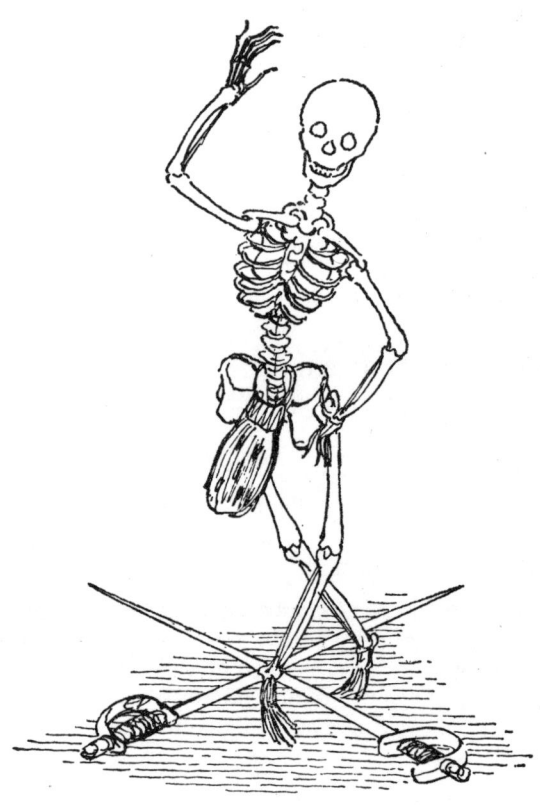

Of Slaves, and Birds, and Animals

BLACK BESS

Dick Turpin, highwayman, was born at Hempstead, Essex, in 1705. He was 'successively and simultaneously' a butcher's apprentice, cattle-lifter, smuggler, house-breaker, highwayman and thief.

To avoid the law, it is said that he rode non-stop from London to York, a distance of around two hundred miles, in sixteen hours. His mare was to become famous as 'Black Bess'.

> From the West was her dam; from the East her sire,
> From the one came her swiftness; the other her fire,
> No peer of the realm better blood can possess,
> Than flows in the blood of my bonny Black Bess.

FROM HENBURY CHURCHYARD, BRISTOL

Here
Lieth the body of
SCIPIO AFRICANUS
Negro servant of the Rt Honourable
Charles William, Earl of Suffolk
and Bristol.
Who died ye 21 Dec, 1720.

THE TOMB OF A FISH
—Blockley, Gloucestershire.

In the memory of the old fish,
Under the soil the old fish do lie,
Twenty year he lived and then did die.
He was so tame you understand,
He would come and eat out of your hand.

Died April the 20th, 1855.

AN UNKNOWN PARTRIDGE
—Northamptonshire.

A Salop Ousley I
a—Partridge wonne
No birds I had her bye
Such work with her was doone
She dead, I turtle sought,
A Wake in Salsir bred
Twice six birds, shee mee brought,
She lyves, but I am dead.
But when ninth year was come
I slept that was A Wake.

SUNDERLAND POINT, LANCASTER

Thoughtless and irreverent people having damaged and defaced the plate, this replica was affixed.

RESPECT THIS LONELY GRAVE.
Here lies
Poor SAMBO
A faithful NEGRO
Who
(Attending his Master from the West Indies)
DIED on his Arrival at SUNDERLAND

Full sixty Years the angry Winters Wave
Has thundering dash'd this bleak & barren Shore.
Since SAMBO's Head laid in this lonely GRAVE
Lies still & ne'er will hear their turmoil more.

76

Full many a Sandbird chirps upon the Sod
And many a Moonlight Elfin round him trips
Full many a Summer's Sunbeam warms the Clod
And many a teeming Cloud upon him drips.

But still he sleeps—till the awakening Sounds
of the Archangel's Trump new life impart
Then the GREAT JUDGE his Approbation sounds
Not on Man's COLOR but his WORTH OF HEART.

H. Bell del.
1796.

SIGNOR FIDO

From a garden formerly belonging to Lord Cobham, at Stow,
Buckinghamshire.

To the memory of
Signor FIDO,
An Italian of good Extraction,
Who came to England,
Not to *bite* us, like most of his Countrymen,
But to gain an honest Livelyhood.
He *hunted* not after Fame,
Yet acquired it.
Regardless of the Praise of his Friends,
But most sensible of their Love.
Tho' he lived among the Great,
He neither learnt nor flatter'd any Vice.
He was no Bigot,
Tho' he doubted of none of the Thirty-nine
Articles:
And if to follow Nature,
And to respect the Laws of Society,
Be Philosophy;
He was a perfect Philosopher,
A faithful Friend,
An agreeable Companion,
A loving husband;
And, tho' an Italian,

Was distinguished by a numerous Offspring:
All which he liv'd to see take good Courses.
In his old age he retir'd
To the house of a Clergyman in the Country,
Where he finish'd his earthly Race,
And died an Honour and Example to the
whole species.
Reader,
This stone is guiltless of Flattery!

WILLIAM HOGARTH'S EPITAPH FOR HIS PET BULLFINCH

Alas poor Dick!
1760
Aged eleven.
(Two cross-bones of birds, over these a heart and a death's
heart.)

ON A GOLDFINCH, BEAUCHAMP TOWER

Buried 23 June 1794 by a fellow-prisoner in the Tower of
London.

Where Raleigh pin'd within a prison's gloom
I cheerful sung, nor murmur'd at my doom
Where heroes bold, and patriots firm could dwell;
A goldfinch in content, his note might swell,
But death, more gentle than the law's decree,
Hath paid my ransom from captivity.

Gems of Wisdom

FROM ESSEX

    When pictures look alive with movements free,
    When ships, like fishes, swim below the sea,
    When men, outstripping birds, can scan the sky,
    Then half the world deep drenched in blood shall lie.

Circa AD 1400.

TRAILFLAT CHURCHYARD

In memory of B.C., died 5 December 1801, aged 64.

    On what a slender thread hangs Everlasting things.

ST MICHAEL'S CHURCHYARD, DUMFRIES

In memory of J.M., died 31 August 1708, aged 50.

    If grace, good manners, gifts of mind,
    Yea where all moral virtues have combined,
    Compleat a man, behold beneath this stone,
    Here lyes interred, whom rich and poor bemoan,
    He run his race, abundant entrance got,
    His name is savori, and shall not rot.

TINWALD CHURCHYARD

T.B., who died 1804.

    That truth how certain when this life is o'er,
    Man dies to live, and lives to die no more.

A SEPTUAGENARIAN'S ADVICE
—Kirkmahoe Churchyard, 1700

> Weep not for me who here do lye,
> Weep for your sins before you dyy,
> For Death is not to be lamented,
> But sin is still to be repented.

ON JOHN ORGONE AND HIS WIFE, ELLYNE, 1584
—St Olave Church, Hart Street.

> As I was, so be ye;
> As I am, you shall be:
> That I gave, that I have;
> That I spent, that I had,
> That I ende all my coste
> That I lefte, that I loste.

FROM WETHERAL

> In this vain world short was my stay,
> And empty was my laughter.
> I go before to clear the way,
> And you'll come jogging after.

*Here lieth the Body
of Joseph Braddick, of
this Parish, who Died
the 27th Day of June, 1673,
in the 40th year of his age.*

Strong and at labour,
Suddenly he reels,
Death came behind him
And stroke up his heels;
Such sudden stroke
Surviving mortals bid ye
Stand on your watch
And to be also ready.

ROBERTUS OF DONCASTER

> How now, who is heare?
> I, Robin of Doncastere,
> And Margaret my feare.

Quoth Robertus Byrks, who in this world did reign three-score years and seven, and yet lived not one.

CREDITON CHURCHYARD

> Why do I live in life a thralle
> of joye and alle berefte?
> Their wings were growne
> to Heaven they're flowne,
> 'Cause I had none I'm lefte.

FROM WAPLEY, GLOUCESTERSHIRE

> A time of death there is
>   you know full well:
> But when, or how 'twill come,
>   no man can tell:
> At midnight, morn, or noon:
>   remember then,
> Death is most certain, though
>   uncertain when.

ST NICHOLAS CHURCH, YARMOUTH

> Here lies a man who first did dye,
> When he was twenty-four,
> And yet he lived to reach the age,
> Of Hoary hairs, fourscore.
> But now he's gone, and certain 'tis
> He'll not dye any more.

ADVICE FROM CHATHAM CHURCHYARD, KENT

> Weep not for him, the warmest tear that's shed
> Falls unavailing o'er the unconscious dead;
> Take the advice these friendly lines would give
> Live not to drink, but only drink to live.

AN EXAMPLE FROM THE NECROPOLIS, GLASGOW

> Stranger as you pass o'er this grass;
> Think seriously, with no humdrumming,
> Prepare for death, for judgement's coming.

A CHURCHYARD IN MANCHESTER

> Here lies John Hill,
> A man of skill,
> His age was five times ten,
> He ne'er did good,
> Nor ever would,
> Had he lived as long again.

FROM LEYLAND CHURCHYARD

> Let the wind go free
> Where'er thou be,
> For twas the wind
> That kill*ed* me.

IT MUST COME

—From the tomb of Mrs Stone, Melton Mowbray churchyard.
> Curious enough, we all must say,
> That what was stone should now be clay;
> Most curious still, to own we must,
> That what was stone must soon be dust.

DEATH OF A WEEK

—St Olave's Churchyard, Southwark.
> Hallowed be the Sabbath
> And farewell all worldly Pelfe,
> The Weeke begins on Tuesday
> For Munday hath hang'd himselfe.

JOHNNIE'S HOPE

—Lincoln Churchyard.
> Here lies John Hyde;
> He first liv'd, and then died;
> He dyed to live, and liv'd to dye,
> And hopes to live eternally.

ON WOMEN

Censure not rashly,
Though nature's apt to halt,
No woman's born,
That dies without a fault.

AN EPITAPH TO BE FOUND ON THE SOUTH WALL OF ELGIN CATHEDRAL, MORAYSHIRE

The world is a city full of streets,
And death the mercat that all men meets,
If lyfe were a thing that monie could bye,
The poor could not live, and the rich would not die.

ADMONISHMENT FROM WORSTEAD CHURCHYARD, NORFOLK

These lines are not to praise the dead
But to admonish those by whom they're read:
Whatever his failings were, leave them alone,
And use thine utmost care to mend thine own.

FROM BROUGHTON, NORTHAMPTONSHIRE

Time was I stood where thou dost now,
And viewed the dead, as thou dost me;
Ere long thou'lt be as low as I,
And others stand and look on thee.

A TOMB NEAR THE CHANCEL DOOR OF GRINDON CHURCH, NEAR LEEK

Farewell, dear friends; to follow me prepare;
Also our loss we'd have you to beware,
And your own business mind. Let us alone,
For you have faults great plenty of your own.
Judge not of us, now we are in our graves
Lest ye be judg'd and awful sentence have;
For backbiters, railers, thieves, and liars,
Must torment have in everlasting fires.

THE MOURNFUL TRUTH

Death comes to all—none can resist his dart,
At his command the dearest friends must part;
A mournful widow, who this truth doth own,
In gratitude erects this humble stone.

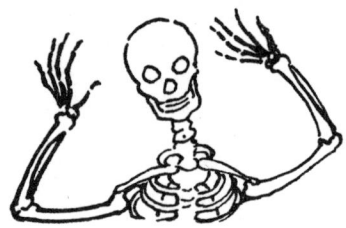

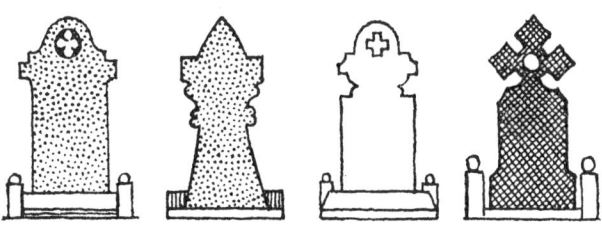

From Distant Lands

FRANCE

MONTMARTRE

Poor CHARLES!
His innocent pleasure was to row on the water.
Alas!
He was the victim of this fatal desire,
Which conducted him to the tomb.
Reader! Consider that the water in which he was drowned
Is the amassed tears of his relatives and friends.

DIJON

The Tomb of Old Le Menestrier.

JEAN LE MENESTRIER lieth here:
Lo! having number'd his seventieth year,
He tightens his stirrups, his spurs he plies,
And starts away for Paradise.

FROM A TOMB IN THE VILLAGE OF AUTHIEUX, NEAR ROUEN

Look, man, before thee, how thy death hasteth;
Look, man, behind thee, how thy life wasteth—
Look on thy right side, how death thee desireth;
Look on thy left side, how sin thee beguileth—
Look, man, above thee, joys that will ever last.
Look, man, beneath thee, the pains without rest.

85

GERMANY

LÜNEBURG, HANOVER

—*The epitaph to a pig on the Hotel de Ville.*

Passer-by, contemplate here the mortal remains of the pig
which acquired for itself imperishable glory by the discovery
of the salt springs of Lüneburg.

ITALY

THE TOMB OF KEATS, ROME

Here lies one whose name is writ in water.

FROM THE CATACOMBS, ROME

HIC VERUS QUI SEMPER VERA LOCUTUS

Here lies Verus [Truth], who always spoke truly.

THE TOMB OF WICKED CHLOË

*IN SCRIPSIT TUMULIS SEPTEM SCELERATA
VIRORUM SE FECISSE
CHLOË, QUID POTE SIMPLICIUS*

Wicked Chloë inscribed on the tombs of her seven
husbands 'I did this'.

N.B. This Latin construction *Chloë fecit*, can mean 'built this
tomb' *and* 'caused the death of'.

FROM FLORENCE

Here lies SALVINO ARMOLO D'ARMATI,
of Florence,
the inventor of spectacles.
May God pardon his sins!
The year 1318.

THE NETHERLANDS

The story goes:

'A man who was very rich, but who was a *bon vivant*, took it into his head that he was to live a certain number of years, and no longer. Under this conviction, he calculated that if he spent so much a year, his estate and his life would expire together. It so happened that he was mistaken in neither of his calculations; he died precisely at the time he had thought he would, and had by then so reduced his fortune that, after paying his debts, there was nothing left but a pair of slippers. His relations buried him in a creditable manner, and had the slippers carved on his tomb with the epitaph:

EFFEN NYT.

Which means "Exactly".'

THE UNITED STATES OF AMERICA

SAN DIEGO

Here lies the body of JEEMS HUMBRICK
who was accidentally shot
on the banks of the Pacus river
by a young man.

He was accidentally shot with one of the large Colt's revolver with no stopper for the cock on it was of the old fashioned kind brass mounted and of such is the Kingdom of Heaven.

ROCKVILLE, MASSACHUSETTS

In memory of JANE BENT,
Who kick'd her heels and away she went.

NEW JERSEY

Reader, pass on, don't waste your time
On bad biography and bitter rhyme:
For what I am, this crumbling clay insures,
And what I was is no affair of yours.

AND FROM THE SAME STATE

JULIA ADAMS,
Died through wearing thin shoes.
April 17th, 1839.
Aged 19 years.

MASSACHUSETTS

I came in the morning—it was Spring,
                    And I smiled;
I walk'd out at noon—it was Summer,
                    And I was glad;
I sat me down at even—it was Autumn,
                    And I was sad;
I laid me down at night—it was Winter,
                    And I slept.

PHILADELPHIA

In memory of HENRY WANG, son of his Father and Mother,
John and Maria Wang. Died Dec. 31st, 1829, aged 1–2 hour.
The first deposit of this yard.

        A short-lived joy
        Was our little boy.
        He has gone on high,
        So don't you cry.

PENNSYLVANIA

Eliza, sorrowing, rears this marble slab
To her dear JOHN, who died of eating crab.

FROM THE CHURCHYARD, SARATOGA SPRINGS

Farewell, dear wife! my life is past;
I loved you while my life did last;
Don't grieve for me, or sorrow take,
But love my brother for my sake.

BURLINGTON CHURCHYARD, IOWA

Beneath this stone our baby lays
He neither cries nor hollers
He lived just one and twenty days,
And cost us forty dollars.

LICHFIELD, CONNECTICUT

Sacred to the memory of inestimable worth, of unrivalled
excellence and virtue ——, whose ethereal parts became
seraphic on the 25th day of May, 1867.

BURLINGTON CHURCHYARD, MASSACHUSETTS

Sacred to the memory of Anthony Drake,
Who died for peace and quietness sake;
His wife was constantly scolding and scoffin',
So he sought for repose in a twelve-dollar coffin.

NEW JERSEY

She was not smart, she was not fair,
But hearts with grief for her are swellin';
And empty stands her little chair:
She died of eatin' water melon.

FROM A CHURCHYARD IN CONNECTICUT

Here lies, cut down like unripe fruit,
The wife of Deacon Amos Shute:
She died of drinking too much coffee,
Anny Dominy eighteen forty.

FROM A GRAVE IN THE WESLEYAN CEMETERY, ST LOUIS

Here lize a stranger braiv,
Who died while fightin' the Suthern Confederacy to save
Piece to his dust.
Brave Suthern friend
From iland 10

You reached a Glory us end.
We plase these flowrs above the stranger's hed,
In honor of the shiverlus ded.
Sweet spirit rest in Heven
Ther'l be know Yankis there.

CONCORD, MASSACHUSETTS

God wills us free—man wills us slaves;
I will as God wills: God will be done.
Here lies the body of
JOHN JACK.
A native of Africa, who died
March 1773, aged about sixty years.
Though born in the land of slavery,
He was born free:
Though he lived in a land of liberty,
He lived a slave:
Till by his honest, though stolen, labours,
He acquired the source of slavery,
Which gave him his freedom:
Though not long before
Death the great Tyrant,
Gave him his final emancipation,
And put him on a footing with kings.
Though a slave to vice.
He practiced those virtues, Without which kings are but
slaves.

CHERAW CHURCHYARD, SOUTH CAROLINA

My name, my country,
What are they to thee?
What, whether high or low,
My pedigree?
Perhaps I far surpassed
All other men:
Perhaps I fall below them all;

What then?
Suffice it, stranger,
Thou see'st a tomb,
Thou know'st its use;
It hides—no matter whom.

AND A MISCELLANY:

Here does the body of MARY ANNE REST,
With her head on Abraham's breast.
It's a very good thing for Mary Anne,
But it's very hard lines on Abraham.

A much esteemed but injudicious man,
Caught a cold in Jan.
He tangled thus in fate's mysterious web,
He died in Feb.

Here lie the remains of poor CHRISTOPHER TYPE,
The rest of him couldn't be found:
He sat on a powder cask, smoking a pipe,
While the wind blew the ashes around.

He scraped away the mossy spray
And scratched amid the lichen green,
Until he read: 'Kate Kelly, dead,
Aged twenty-seven. Kerosene.'

He turned the corner with a moan,
By thirst for knowledge goaded,
And found another stone:
'Didn't know 'twas loaded.'

Here lies the Reverend Johnathan Doe,
Where he's gone to I don't know.
If haply to the realms above,
Farewell to happiness and love.
If, haply to a lower level,
I can't congratulate the Devil.

EPITAPH FROM INDIA

Sacred to the Memory of
The Rev ——
Who, after twenty year's unremitting labour
as a Missionary
Was accidently shot by his native bearer.
'WELL DONE THOU GOOD AND FAITHFUL SERVANT.'

EPITAPH FROM GREECE

Sardanapalus' Tomb.

SARDANAPALUS, son of Anacyndaraxes, caused the towns of Auchiales and Tarsus to be built in a single day. Pass on stranger. Eat, drink, and enjoy yourself, for nought else is worth a fillip.

EPITAPH FROM AUSTRALIA

GOD took our flower—our little Nell,
He thought He too would like a smell.

THE JAPANESE WAY OF EPITAPHS

Japan and her people never cease to be an enigma to the Western mind. While, on the one hand, the tourist can see new and efficient factories growing up, on the other he can see in the grounds of these factories special shrines for the souls of broken nails, or sewing-machine needles.

The whole length of Japan is covered with epitaphs and shrines of one kind or another. In the city of Kyoto, there is an important shrine to TAJIMAMORI-NO-MIKOTO, which has a 2,000-year-old legend about confectionery. The Emperor Siunin sent Taji to China with a command to bring back some *kashi*, or iced toffee. Taji returned sixteen years later, by which time the Emperor had died. Taji was very upset and, considering that he had insulted the Emperor, he committed *seppuku*—a more polite way of saying *hara-kiri*. Today the shrine to Taji is visited regularly by confectioners from all over Japan.

You name it and the Japanese have a shrine for it!

From Tinker and Tailor to Soldier and Sailor

THOMAS THE WIGMAKER, OBIT 1735, AND HIS WIFE
—St Michael's Churchyard, Dumfries.

Two lovers true for ten years' space absented,
By stormy seas, and wars, yet liv'd contented,
We met for eighteen years, and married were.
God smil'd on us, our wind bleue always fair,
We're ancor'd here, waiting our Master's call,
Expecting with Him, joys perpetuall.

THE RECUSANTS
—Wigtown Churchyard.

Here lyes William Johnston, John Milroy, George
Walker, who was, without sentence of Law, hanged by
Major Winram for their adherence to Scotland's Reforma-
tion Covenant National and Solemn League, 1685.

THE TOWN DRUMMER
—Langholm Churchyard.

Interred here, Archibald Beattie, town drummer, who
for more than half a century kept up the ancient and annual
custom of proclaiming the Langholm Fair at the Cross
when riding the common granted to the town, and pointing

out to the inhabitants thereof the various boundaries of those rights which descended from their ancestors to posterity. He died in 1823, aged 90 years. The managers of the Common-Riding for the year 1829 have caused his name to be here inscribed, as a tribute of respect due to his memory.

THE MURDERED PEDLAR
—Eskdalemuir Churchyard.

In memory of John Elliot, Pedlar, a young man of 19 years of age, who came from the neighbourhood of Hexham, in Northumberland, and travelling in company with a man of the name of James Gordon, said to have come from Mayo, was barbarously murdered by him at Steelebush-edge, on the farm of Upper Cassock, on the 14th day of November, 1820.

After the greatest exertions on the part of Sir Thomas Kirkpatrick, of Closeburn, Bart, Sheriff-Depute of the County, the Hon Captain Wm Napier of Thirlstane, and many others, the above-named Jas Gordon was apprehended at Nairn, and brought to Dumfries, where, after an interesting trial, he was condemned, and executed on the 6th day of June, 1821.

The inhabitants of Eskdalemuir, in order to convey to future ages their abhorrence of a crime which was attended with peculiar aggravations, and their veneration for those laws which pursue with equal solicitude the murderer of a poor, friendless stranger, as of a peer of the realm, have erected this stone, 1st September, 1821.

THE WOOL DRESSER
—Dundee.

Here lie the banes o' Tammas Messer,
Of tarry woo he was a dresser:
He had some faults and mony merits,
And died o' drinking ardent spirits.

THE DOCTOR'S EPITAPH
—Castleton Churchyard.

John Armstrong, M.D., born 1709, died 1779.
If yet thy shade delights to hover near
The holy ground, where oft thy sire hath taught,
And where our fathers fondly flocked to hear;
Accept the offering which their sons have brought.
Proud of the muse, which gave to classic fame,
Our vale and stream, to song before unknown,
We raise this stone to bear thy deathless name
And tell the world that Armstrong was our own,
To learning worth and genius, such as thine,
How vain the tribute monuments can pay!
Thy name immortal with thy works shall shine,
And live where frailer marbles shall decay.

THE CARRIER'S STORY
—Kilbride Churchyard.

Here lye the banes of Thamas Tyre,
Wha lang had trudged thro' dub and mire,
In carrying bundles and sic like,
His task performing wi' sma' fyke.
To deal in snuff he aye was free,
And served his friends for little fee,
His life obscure was naething new,
Yet we must own his faults were few.
Although at Yule he sipped a drap,
And in the kirk whiles took a nap,
True to his work in every case
Tam scorned to cheat for lucre base;
Now he has gone to taste the fare
Which only honest men will share.

95

THE HAMPSHIRE GRENADIER
—Winchester Cathedral.

In memory of
THOMAS THATCHER

A grenadier in the North Regt of Hants Militia, who died of a violent fever contracted by drinking small beer when hot, the 12th of May 1764. Aged 26 years. In grateful remembrance of whose universal good will towards his comrades, this stone is placed here at the expence as a small testimony of their regard and concern.

Here sleeps in peace a Hampshire Grenadier,
Who caught his death by drinking cold small beer;
Soldiers, be wise from his untimely fall,
And when you're hot drink strong, or none at all.

EPITAPH FOR AN ARCHITECT

In the churchyard of Sarnesfield, near Weobley, Herefordshire, there is a very unusual epitaph to John Abel, the architect of the market-houses of Hereford, Knighton, Brecknock and Leominster, who died in 1694. On the stone are to be found three figures kneeling, Abel and his two wives. On this stone are also the tools of Abel's trade.

This craggy stone a covering is for an architect's bed;
That lofty building raisèd high, yet now lies low his head;
His line and rule, so death concludes, are lockèd up in store;
Build they who list, or they who wist, for he can build no
    more.

His house of clay could hold no longer, May Heaven's joy
build him a stronger. JOHN ABEL.

Vive ut vivas in vitam aeternam.

THE PEDLAR'S EPITAPH
—Troutbeck, Westmorland.

If Bowness village you should know,
There may you hear my fyles to go,
Pins and needles, sirs, who buyes 'em,
Hard and sharp, whoever tryes 'em,
Toys and rattles to still babyes,
Temple wires, that's fit for ladyes.
Come and buy, if you'll have any,
I wod fain draw the packing penny.
Whilst the pedlar thus doth bawle,
And his wares for sale doth call,
Death passes by like one unknown,
Commands him pack—his market's done.

THE DIRECTOR'S STONE IN CHELSEA OLD CHURCH

Here lies the body of Mr Francis
Thomas, Director of the China
Porcelain, Manufactory, Lawrence
Street, Chelsea. Departed this life
Between the hours of ten and eleven
o'clock, Sunday night the 6th of
January, 1770, in the 45th year of his
age. Surely the tenderest husband,
The best of fathers, and the sincerest friend,
Whose death is greatly lamented by us all and his
friends.

Oh! but when the great God does call,
And summons us both great and small,
Therefore let us, my friends, prepare,
Like this, the best of Fathers here.

THE MAJOR OF HIGH WYCOMBE

Here lies removed from mundane scenes,
A major of the King's Marines,
Under arrest in narrow borders,
He rises not till further orders.

PEPPER'S GRAVE
—St John's Church, Stamford.

On William Pepper,
Tho' hot my name, yet mild my nature,
I bore goodwill to every creature,
I brewed good ale, and sold it too,
And unto each I gave his due.

SMITH, THE HABERDASHER

Here lies John Smith, sometime Hosier and Haberdasher
in this Town.
He left his hose, his Anna and his love,
To sing Hosanna in the realms above.

ON AN OLD SOLDIER'S GRAVE

God and our soldier we alike adore,
Just at the brink of danger, not before:
After the battle they're alike requited,
God is forbidden and the soldier slighted.

IN MEMORY OF WILLIAM RICHARD PHÉLPS, LATE BOAT-SWAIN OF HMS 'INVINCIBLE'

He accompanied Lord Anson on his cruise round the world, and died 21 April 1789.

When I was like you,
For years, not a few,
On the ocean I toil'd,
On the line I have broil'd,

In Greenland I've shiver'd,
Now from hardships deliver'd,
Capsized by old Death
I surrender'd my breath,
And now I lie snug
As a bug in a rug.

THE MEMORIAL BRASS OF AN MP IN RYE CHURCH, SUSSEX

Loe Thomas Hamon here enter'd doth lye,
Thrice Burgesse for the Parliament elected,
Six times by freemen's choyce made Maior of Rye,
And Captaine longe time of the band selected
Whose prudent courage, justice, gravitie
Deserves a monument of memorye.
Died 1607.

LINES ON A WAGGONER'S TOMB
—Bisbrooke Churchyard.

Here lies the body of Nathaniel Clarke,
Who never did no harm in the light, nor in the dark,
But in his blessed horses, taking great delight,
And often travelled with them by day and by night.

THE ROADMENDER
—St Edith's Churchyard, Eaton-under-Heywood, Shropshire.

Thomas Corfield, the author and Sole cause of
Mending the roads in his (bad) very bad neighbour-wood.

THE ZEALOUS LOCKSMITH

A zealous locksmith dy'd of late,
And did arrive at Heaven's gate,
He stood without and would not knock,
Because he meant to pick the lock.

CRUMMY ABERCROMBIE OF THE PENNY WHISTLE

Here Crummy lies, enclosed in wood,
Full six feet one and better,
When tyrant Death grim o'er him stood,
He faced him like a hatter.
Now lies he low without a boot,
Free from this world of bustle,
And silent now is Crummy's flute,
And awful dry his whustle.

A PAUPER'S GRAVE

Poorly lived,
And poorly died,
Poorly buried,
And no one cried.

FROM LOGIEPERT CHURCHYARD, NEAR MONTROSE, ANGUS

Here lies the Smith—to wit—Tam Gouk,
His Faither and his Mither,
Wi Tam, and Jock, and Joan and Noll,
And a' the Gouks thegither.
When on the yird Tam and his wife
'Greed desperate ill wi'ither,
But noo, without e'en din or strife
They tak' their Nap thegither.

THE TREASURER OF ARBROATH

Here lyes Alexander Peter, who died 12th January, 1630.
Such a Treasurer was not since, nor yet before,
For common work, calsais [causeways], brigs [bridges],
    and schoir [sewers],
Of all others he did excel;
He devised our school and he hung our bell.

TO A SAILOR BENEFACTOR
—Deskford Churchyard, near Cullen.

Hic jacet Joannes Anderson, Aberdoniensis,
  Who built this churchyard dyke at his own expences.

A SEXTON'S STORY

Hurra! my brave boys,
Let's rejoice at his fall!
For if he had lived,
He had buried us all.

THE MERCHANT

The epitaph of JOHN PHILIPS, Chester Cathedral.

Here lies a marchand who on earth did trade
To gaine a Kingdome that should never fade.
An upright conscience his best chosen Frend
Did steere his shipp unto his latest end,
Till here arivd in Heaven with God his maker,
Who now of endless Joyes is made Partaker.
He led a life scarce blemished with one staine,
Beloved of all & loving all againe,
Upon Good Friday he with Christ did die,
That hee with Him might live eternally.

THE CLERGYMAN FROM CORK

RICHARD BOARDMAN
Departed this life October 4th, 1782.
Aetatis 44.

Beneath this stone the dust of BOARDMAN lies,
His precious soul has soar'd above the skies;
With eloquence divine, he preach'd the word
To multitudes, and turned them to the Lord.
His bright example strengthened what he taught,
And devils trembled when for Christ he fought.
With truly Christian zeal he nations fired,
And all who knew him mourn'd when he expired.

LINES ON A SMUGGLER

Here I lies,
Killed by the X.I.S.

THE WATCHMAKER FROM BOLSOVER, DERBYSHIRE

Here lieth, in a horizontal position,
The outsize case of THOMAS HINDE,
Clock and Watchmaker.

Who departed this life, wound up in hope of being taken
in hand by his Maker, and being thoroughly cleaned,
repaired, and set a-going in the world to come. On the
15th day of August 1836.

FROM WIRKSWORTH

Near this place the body of
PHILIP SHULLCROSS

Once eminent Quill-driver to the attorneys in this Town.
He died the 17th Nov, 1787, Aged 67.

Viewing Philip in a moral light, the most Prominent and
remarkable features in his character were his zeal and in-
vincible attachment to dogs and cats, and his unbounded
benevolence towards them, as well as towards his fellow-
creatures.

TO THE CRITIC

Seek not to show the devious paths Phil trode,
Nor tear his frailties from their dread abode,
In modest sculpture let this tombstone tell,
That much esteem'd he lived, and much regretted fell.

THE BLACKSMITH'S EPITAPH

This epitaph, written by the poet Hayley, has proved a
favourite with blacksmiths. Among other places it appears in
the churchyards of Rochdale, Bothwell, Feltham and Westham.

My sledge and hammer lie declined,
My bellows-pipes have lost their wind,
My fire's extinct, my forge decay'd,
My vice is in the dust now laid;
My coal is spent, my iron's gone,
My nails are drove, my work is done,
My fire-dried corpse here lies at rest,
My soul, smoke-like, soars to be blest.

ST DUNSTAN'S CHURCHYARD, STEPNEY

Here lies the body of Daniel Saul,
Spittlefield's weaver and that's all.

THE MILKMAN OF EARLS BARTON, NORTHANTS

A milkman's tomb.
Milk and water sold I ever,
Weight and measure, gave I never,
So, to the devil I must go,
Woe, woe, woe, woe.

THE ATTORNEY
—Castleton, in the Peak District.

To
The memory of
MICAH HALL, Gentleman,
Attorney at Law,
Who died on the 14th of May, 1804,
Aged 79 years.

Quid eran nescitis;	What I was you know not;
Quid sum, nescitis;	What I am you know not;
Ubi abii, nescitis;	Whither I am gone you know not;
Valete.	Farewell.

THE DAIRYMAN'S DAUGHTER
—Church of Mount Jerome, Dublin.

This lonely bud, so young and fair,
Call'd hence by early doom,
Just came to show how sweet a flower
In Paradise might bloom.

A HENPECKED CLOCKMAKER

Here lies a mon, who all his mortal life
Passed mending clocks, but could not mend his wife.
The 'larum of his bell was ne'er sae shrill
As was her tongue, aye clacking like a mill.
But now he's gane—on, wither? nane can tell—
I hope beyond the sound of O'Mally's bell.

FROM REDKIRK IN THE PARISH OF GRETNA

The sea swept the churchyard away but left this stone high
and dry.

Here lieth I—N BELL, who died in ye yhere MDX, and
his age CXXX years. Here bluidy Bell, baith skin and bane,
lies quietly styll beneath this stane; He was a stark moss-
trooper shent as ever drave a bow on bent. He brynt ye
Lockwood tower and hall. An' flang ye lady o'er ye wall;
For whilk a Johnstone, stout and wyte; Set Blacketh & in
low by nicht, Whyle cryed a voice, as if frae Hell, 'Haste,
open ye gates for bluidy Bell.'

THE TOMB OF A SAILOR AND HIS WIFE
—St Andrew's, near St Regulus Tower.

Here we lie
In horizontal position,
Like a ship laid up
Stript of her mast and riggin'.

THE PORTSMOUTH CARPENTER

Here lies JEMMY LITTLE, a carpenter industrious,
A very good-natured man, but somewhat blusterous.
When that his little wife his authority withstood,
He took a little stick and bang'd her as he would.
His wife, now left alone, her loss does so deplore,
She wishes JEMMY back to bang her a little more;
For now he's dead and gone this fault appears so small,
A little thing would make her think it was no fault at all.

THE EPITAPH OF JOSEPH BLACKETT, POET AND SHOE-MAKER OF SEAHAM, DURHAM

Written by Lord Byron.

OBIT 1810.

Stranger! behold interr'd together
The *souls* of learning and of leather.
Poor Joe is gone, but left his *awl*—
You'll find his relics in a *stall*.
His work was neat, and often found
Well-stitched and with morocco bound.
Tread lightly—where the bard is laid
He cannot mend the shoe he made;
Yet he is happy in his hole
With verse immortal as his *sole*.
But still to business he held fast,
And stuck to Phoebus to the last.
Then who shall say so good a fellow
Was only leather and prunella?
For character—he did not lack it,
And if he did—'twere shame to *Black-it*!

TO ADAMS, THE CARRIER
—Southwell Churchyard, Nottingham.

JOHN ADAMS lies here, of the parish of Southwell,
A carrier who carried his can to his mouth well;
He carried it much and he carried it fast,

He could carry no more—so was carried at last:
For the liquor, being too much for one,
He could carry off—so he's now carri-on.

THE ORGANIST AND THE BELLOWS-MAKER
—Oxford.

Here lies one MEREDITH, Organist, blown out of breath,
Who lived a merry life, and died a Merideth.

Here lyeth JOHN CRUCKER, a maker of bellows,
His crafts-master and king of good fellows:
Yet when he came to the hour of his death,
He that made bellows could not make breath.

A RARE TALE

Here lies PARKET HALL, an what is more rarish,
He was born, bred, and hung in St Thomas's parish.

THE FLUTIST OF KINNOUL

Halt for a moment,
Passenger, and read.
Here Andrew dozes
In his daisied bed.

Silent his flute,
Torn off its key,
His genius scattered
And the Muse set free.

JOCK THE MASON
—The Abbey Churchyard, Melrose.

JOHN MURDO som tym callit was i,
And born in Parysse certainly,
And had in kepying all mason werk
Of Sanctandroys, the hye kirk.

Of Glasgu, Melros, and Paslay,
Of Nyddysdale, and of Galway,
Pray to God, and Mari baith,
And sweet St John, keep this holy kyrk fra skaith.

TO JOHN SPONG, CARPENTER
—Ockham Churchyard, Woking.

Who many a sturdy oak had laid along,
Fell'd by Death's surer hatchet here lies Spong.
Posts oft he made, yet ne'er a place could get,
And lived by railing, though he was no wit;
Old saws he had, although no antiquarian,
And stiles corrected, yet was no grammarian.

ST JULIAN'S CHURCHYARD, SHREWSBURY

The remains of HENRY COOPER of this parish, Chirurgeon, who deceased April 11, 1691, and Annie his wife, who followed him the next day after:

We man and wife,
Conjoined for life,
Fetched our last breath
So near that Death,
Who parted us would,
Yet hardly could,
Wedded againe,
In bed of dust,
Here we remain,
Till rest we must.
A double prize this grave doth finde,
If you are wise keep it in minde.

THE HIGHWAYMAN FROM NAYLAND

Here sleepeth in dust,
NED ALSTON,
The notorious Essex Highwayman,
Ob. Anno Dom, 1760.
Aetat 40.

107

My friends, here I am—Death at last has prevail'd,
And for once all my projects are baffled,
'Tis a blessing to know, tho', when once a man's nail'd,
He has no further dread of the scaffold.
My life was cut short by a shot thro' the head,
On his Majesty's highway at Dalston—
So as now 'Number One' numbered one of the dead,
All's one if he's Alston or All-stone.

THE DUNMORE GROCER
—County Waterford.

Here lie the remains of JOHN HALL, grocer,
The world is not worth a fig, and
I have good raisins for saying so.

A SMALLTIME SHOPKEEPER
—Wigtown Churchyard.

Here lies John Taggart, of honest fame,
Of stature low, and a leg lame;
Content he was with portion small,
Kept a shop in Wigtown, and that's all.

THE TOMB OF AN ENGINE-DRIVER
—Broomsgrove Churchyard.

My engine now is cold and still,
No water does my boiler fill,
My coke affords its flame no more:
My days of usefullness are o'er:
My whistle, too, has lost its tune,
Its shrill and thrilling sounds are gone:
My valves are now thrown open wide:
My flanges all refuse to glide,
Life's railway o'er, each station's passed,
In death I'm stopped, and rest at last,
Farewell, dear friends, and cease to weep:
In Christ I'm safe: in Him I sleep.

108

UPTON-ON-SEVERN CHURCHYARD

Beneath this stone in hopes of Zion,
Doth lie the landlord of the Lion;
His son keeps on the business still,
Resigned upon the heavenly will.

ANOTHER INNKEEPER FROM BELBOROUGH

Of all the epitaphs of innkeepers, perhaps this is the most
ornate. The upper part of the tombstone is carved with a punch-
bowl, bottles and pots in full relief.

To RICHARD PHILPOTS, Keeper of the Bell Inn.
Died 1766.

To tell a merry or a wondrous tale
Over a cheerful glass of nappy ale,
In harmless mirth was his supreme delight,
To please his guests or friends by day or night.
But no fine tale, how well soever told,
Could make the tyrant Death his stroke withhold,
That fatal stroke had laid him here in dust,
To rise again once more with joy we trust.

AND TWO FOR THE ROAD

Hic Jacet WALTER GUN,
Sometime landlord of the 'Sun'.
Sic transit gloria mundi!
He drank hard upon Friday,
This being a high day,
Took to his bed,
And died upon Sunday.

In the year of Our
Lord, 1740
I came to 'The
Crown',
In 1791 they laid me
down.

TWO LAYS FROM SELBY ABBEY

Slab epitaph of John Edmonds, mariner, 5 August 1767.

Tho' Boreas with his blust'ring blasts,
Has tost me to and fro,
Yet by the handywork of God,

I'm here inclos'd below.
And in this silent bay I lie
With many of our fleet,
Untill the day that I set sail,
My Admiral Christ to meet.

John Archer, Sexton, Died 15th Sept, 1786, Aged 74.

Near to this stone lies Archer (John)
    Late Saxton (I aver)
Who, without tears, thirty-four years
    Did carcases inter.

But, Death at last, for his work's past,
    Unto him thus did say:
'Leave off thy trade, be not afraid,
    But forthwith come away.'

Without reply or asking why,
    The summons he obey'd,
In seventeen hundred and sixty-eight,
    Resigned his life and spade.

ON A BOOKSELLER

Here lies poor NED PARDON, from misery freed,
Who long was a bookseller's hack;
He led such a damnable life in this world,
I don't think he'll ever come back.

ON AN EDITOR

Here lies an editor!
Snooks if you will;
In mercy, Kind Providence,
Let him lie still!
He lied for his living: so
He lived while he lied:
When he could not lie longer,
He lied down and died.

A PRINTER'S EPITAPH

No more shall copy bad perplex my brain:
No more shall type's small face my eye-balls strain;
No more the proof's foul page create me troubles,
By errors, transpositions, outs and doubles;
No more my head shall ache from author's whims,
And over-runnings, driving-outs and ins,
The surly pressman's frown I now may scoff
Revised, corrected, finally wrought off.

JOHN BROWN, THE DENTIST

Stranger! Approach this spot with gravity!
John Brown is filling his last cavity.

THE CAPTAIN'S LAST VOYAGE

At anchor now in Death's dark road,
Rides honest Captain Hill,
Who served his King and feared his God,
With upright heart and will.
In social life sincere and just,
To vice of no kind given;
So that his better part, we trust,
Hath made the Port of Heaven.

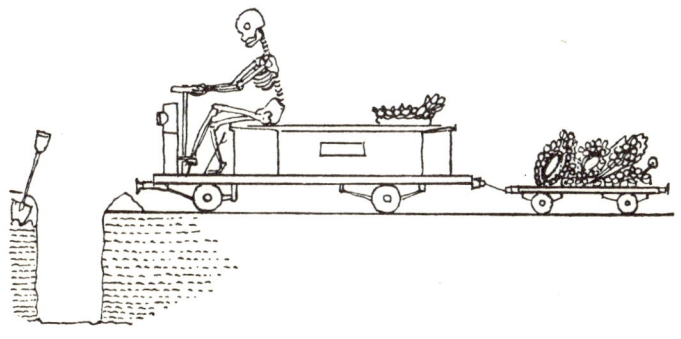

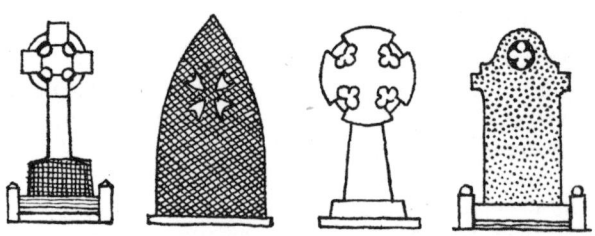

Pluto's Favourite Miscellany

A COLLECTION OF EPITAPHS FROM ALL OVER THE BRITISH ISLES

> Reader of these four lines take heed,
> And mend your life for my sake:
> For you must die, like ISAAC REED,
> Tho' you *read* till your eyes ache!

> Grim death took me without any warning,
> I was well at night, and dead at nine in the morning.

Here lies the body of

JOHN PARTRIDGE

Who departed this life, July 24th ——

> 'Oh, Death, fie, fie,
> To kill a partridge in July.'

> Here lies the body of Margaret Crowther,
> Who died through drinking a seidlitz-powder.
> Oh! may her soul in Heaven be blessed:
> But she should have waited till it effervessed.

Beneath the gravel and these stones,
Lie poor JACK TIFFEY's skin and bones;
His flesh, I often heard him say,
He hoped in time would make good hay;
Quoth I, 'How can that come to pass?'
And he replied, 'All flesh is grass.'

Hurrah! my boys, at the Parson's fall,
For if he'd lived he'd buried us all.

THE ORGAN BLOWER

Under this stone lies Meredith Morgan,
Who blew the bellows of our church organ.
Tobacco he hated, to smoke most unwilling,
Yet never so pleased as when pipes he was filling.
No reflection on him for rude speech could be cast,
Though he gave our old organ many a blast!
No puffer was he, though a capital blower;
He could blow double C, and now lies a note lower.

MARTHA SNELL AND ANN MANN

Poor Martha Snell! her's gone away,
Her would if her could, but her couldn't stay;
Her'd two sore legs and a baddish cough,
But her legs it was as carried her off.

Here lies Ann Mann;
She lived an old Maid,
And she died an old Mann.

GREEDY TAM REID

Here lies Tam Reid,
Who was chokit deid, Wi' taking a feed,
O'butter and breed, Wi' owre muckle speed, When he had
     nae need,
          But just for greed.

MAIDS, HUSBANDS AND WIVES

This spot is the sweetest I've seen in my life,
For it raises my flowers and covers my wife.

Beneath this silent stone is laid,
A noisy, antiquated maid.
Who from her cradle talk'd till death,
And ne'er before was out of breath.

Here lies in silent clay,
MISS ARABELLA YOUNG,
Who on the 21st of May,
Began to hold her tongue.

Here lies the body of JOHN MOUND,
Who was lost at sea and never found.

Here lies DONALD,
And his wife JANET MACFEE,
           Aged 40 hee,
           And 30 shee.

This turf has drunk a widow's tear,
Three husbands are buried here.

God works a wonder now and then,
He, though a lawyer, was an honest man.

Death will'd that WILLING here should lie,
Although unwilling he to die.

ANTIQUARIAT

From time to time cryptic archaic epitaphs have given scholars some headaches. This was no exception, and after many local antiquarians and archaeologists had deliberated on it to no avail, it was translated by a schoolboy.

BENE
A.TH. TH ISST Onere.
Pos. Et. H. CLAUD . COS
TER. Trip. E. Sellero.
F. IMP.
IN GT . Onas DO .
TH. HI S.C.
On. S Or . T. Iane.

Translation:
Beneath this stone reposeth CLAUD COSTER, tripeseller of
Impington, as doth his consort, Jane.

Certainly this is comparable with the epitaph Mr Pickwick
found on his travels.

+

BILST
UM
PSHI
S.M.
ARK.

Translation:

+

BILL STUMPS . HIS MARK.

A MISCELLANY

Here lies a poor woman who always was tired,
She lived in a house where no help was hired.
The last words she said were 'Dear friends I am going,
Where washing an't wanted, nor mending, nor sewing.
Where all things is done just exact to my wishes,
For where folks don't eat there's no washing of dishes.
In Heaven loud anthems for ever are ringing,
But having no voice, I'll keep clear of singing.
Don't mourne for me now, don't mourne for me never;
I'm going to do nothing for ever and ever.

Here lies, thank God, a woman who
Quarrelled and stormed her whole life through:
Tread gently o'er her mouldering form,
Or else you'll arouse another storm.

Erected to the memory of Mr Johnathan Gill
            who died Febr 6, 1751.
Aged 45 years and 6 months.

Beneath this smooth stone,
By the bone of his bone,
Sleeps Mr Johnathan Gill,
By lies when alive this
Attorney did thrive,
And now that he's dead he
            lies still.

Here lies Fred,
Who was alive, and is dead.
Had it been his father
I had much rather:
Had it been his mother,
Better than another:
Had it been his sister,
No one would have missed her:
Had it been his entire generation,
So much the better for the nation:
But since 'tis only Fred,
Who was alive, and is dead,
There's no more to be said.

The epitaph of Coleman the Jesuit, who was hanged in the
reign of Charles II.

If Heaven be pleased when sinners cease to sin,
If Hell be pleased when souls are damned therein,
If Earth be pleased when it's rid of a knave,
Then all are pleased, for Coleman's in his grave.

TO AN ANGLER

He angled many a purling brook,
But lacked the angler's skill:
He lied about the fish he took,
And here he's lying still.

TO THE HUSBANDS OF IVY SAUNDERS

1790. 1794. 1808. 18—.
Here lies my husbands, One, Two, Three.
    Dumb as men could ever be
As for my Fourth, well, praise be God
He bides for a little above the sod.
    Alex, Ben, Sandy were the
        First three names
        And to make things tidy
        I'll add his —— James.

TO FREDERICK TWITCHELL

Dep June 11 . 1811 .
Aged 24 yrs, 5 mos.
Here lie the bones of Lazy Fred,
Who wasted precious time in bed.
Some plaster fell down on his head,
    And thanks be praised—Our
        Freddie's dead.

TOO MUCH AND TOO LATE

Here lies I and my three daughters,
Killed by drinking Cheltenham waters,
If we'd kept to Epsom Salts,
We wouldn't be lying in these 'ere vaults.

Here lies the Mother of Twenty-eight,
It might have been more, but now it's too late.

FLYING HIGHER

There was an old man who averred,
He had learned how to fly like a bird,
Cheered by thousands of people,
He leapt from the steeple—
This tomb states the date it occurred.

There was a young girl in the choir,
Whose voice arose higher and higher,
Till one Sunday night,
It rose quite out of sight,
And they found it next day on the spire.

FROM BUN TO BULL

Here lies John Bun,
He was killed by a gun.
His name was not Bun but Wood,
But Wood would not rhyme with Gun,
        but Bun would.

Here lies the Laird O'Lundie,
Sic transit gloria mundi.

In a vault underneath,
Lie several of the Saunderses,
Late of the Parish—particulars
The last day will disclose.

As I was a riding along the road
Not knowing what was coming,
A bull all horned, and pursued,
After me came a running;
He with his horns struck at me
He being sore offended,
I, from my horse, was forced to fall,
And so my days were ended.

IN A FEW WORDS

Aspice

Respice   Prospice.

—Stepney Churchyard.

Here lies the wife of Simon Stokes.
Who lived and died like other folks.

THE EPITAPH OF CHARLES KNIGHT:

Good Knight.

THE CONDUCTOR

Stephen and Time are now both even;
Stephen beat Time—now Time beat Stephen.

ANN SHORT

A m Short, O Lord, of praising thee,
N othing I can do is right;
N eedy and naked, poor be I,
S hort, Lord, I am of sight;
H ow short I am of love and grace!
O f everything I'm short
R enew me, then I'll follow peace
T hrough good and bad report.

STEPHEN REMNANT

Here's a Remnant of life, and a Remnant of death,
Taken off both at once in Remnant of breath;
To mortality this gives a happy release,
For what the Remnant proves now the whole piece.

JOHN ADAMS

Here lies JOHN ADAMS, who received a thump,
Right on the forehead, from the parish pump,
Which gave him the quietus in the end,
For many doctors did his case attend.

OLD JOHN HILDIBRODD

Here lies old John Hildibrodd,
Have mercy on him, Good God,
As he would if he was God,
And Thou wer't old John Hildibrodd.

WRITTEN BY HIMSELF

Here lies John So,
(So so did he so),
So did he live,
So did he die,
So so did he so,
So let him die.

ON HUSBAND AND WIFE

Here lies the body of JAMES ROBERTSON, and RUTH his
wife.
'Their warfare is accomplished.'

A TROUBLESOME WIFE

Here lies my wife in earthly mould,
Who, when she liv'd naught did but scold;
Peace, wake her not, for now she's still,
She had, but now I have my will.

A QUICK DEMISE

Sudden and unexpected was the end,
Of our esteemed and beloved friend,
He gave to all his friends a sudden shock,
By one day falling into Sunderland dock.

FROM GUNWALLOW CHURCHYARD, NEAR HELSTON, CORN-
WALL

Shall	weee	all	die?
Weee	shall	die	all.
All	die	shall	weee?
Die	all	weee	shall.

HIC JACET

```
        I ...  5 - 4,
O ...  4 ...  I ...  2 ...  8,
O ...  4 ...  I ...  2 ...  O,
O ...  2 ... 80 ...  8,
O ...  2 ... 45 ...  4.
```

LLOUGHOR CHURCHYARD, GLAMORGANSHIRE

This epitaph tells of the custom of funeral garlands which
were strewn on the graves of young unmarrieds every year. The
custom was not peculiar to Wales; it was to be found particularly in Derbyshire.

The village maidens to her grave shall bring,
Selected garlands each returning spring;
Selected sweets, in emblem of the maid
Who underneath this hallow'd turf is laid:
Like her they flourish, beauteous to the eye;
Like her, too soon they languish, fade and die.

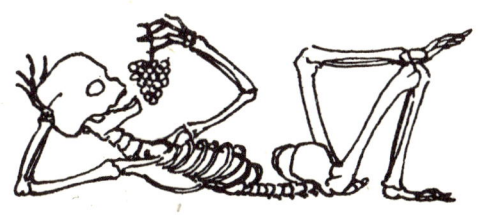

121

ENVOY

After reading through what must amount to thousands of epitaphs, I think, in this day and age, that this is perhaps the finest:

'He was a man.'

Index

Also for the churchyard visitor:

CHURCH FURNITURE

by

Eric R. Delderfield

This is not an exhaustive book of reference but the plain man's guide to the things to be found in and around almost any parish church, large or small. Alphabetically arranged and lavishly illustrated, it will help anyone to find, identify and pass judgment on both the ordinary things and the unique and beautiful things to be seen in even the briefest of visits.

Most of us sometimes glance quickly inside the church when passing through a town or village new to us. But though we may look up and admire the roof or comment that the pews look old, we have little idea of what detailed equipment the church may contain or its history purpose. What are those alcoves for, and when would those carvings have been put there? Why does this church have a stone altar when the last town's had a wooden one? This pulpit looks unusual, but why and how? What is that thing called and what is it for? Are there any other tombs like this?

The author clearly describes each item and sets it in its place in history, mentioning examples to be seen in particular churches. The periods in the past when much building and equipping of churches was going on are identified, and the effects of the Reformation upheaval on what we see today are indicated. There is a full and useful index, and for those who would like to know more about what they see there is a list of books for further reading.

32 pages of plates   *Paperback 5s*   *Hard covers 21s*

DAVID & CHARLES
NEWTON ABBOT